MEL BAY PRESENTS

MASTER ANTHOLOGY
OF FINGERSTYLE GUITAR SOLOS

VOLUME

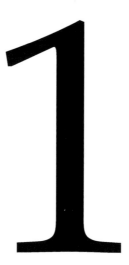

1 2 3 4 5 6 7 8 9 0

Contents

Contents

Jonathan Adams

The stunning virtuosity of Jonathan Adams has inspired and entertained a wide variety of enthusiastic audiences across the country. As a boy Adams' artistic curiosity was initially sparked by his father's study of the acoustic guitar. Although he began with the popular fingerstyle technique of the day, the guitarist was soon drawn to the intimate beauty and diversity of the classical repertoire.

Adams' studies eventually took him to the University of Georgia where he was privileged to study with the renowned John Sutherland. Along with refining his fluid technique, the musician was encouraged by Sutherland to follow his own artistic sensibilities and to expand the diverse repertoire of the guitar.

In addition to his studies with Sutherland, Adams had the rare opportunity to perform in masterclasses under the direction of one of the world's preeminent virtuosos of the classic guitar, Christopher Parkening. The eloquent musicianship of the Maestro is so clearly evident in his student. Adams' talent was such that he was invited by the class to represent his peers in a live interview and performance that was broadcast on public radio.

Adams released his first independent recording *Jonathan Adams: Guitarist* to critical acclaim. He recorded an album of classic guitar favorites for Intersound International the following year. In addition to his exciting recordings for the solo guitar, Jonathan has also written articles and arrangements for *Fingerstyle Guitar Magazine* and Mel Bay Publications.

Adams' unique ability to communicate the works of classical composers is only bested by his warmth and personality. From Bach to the Beatles, his arrangements and original compositions have expanded the repertoire of the guitar with flair and creativity not often experienced. Intensely talented and incredibly polished, Adams' light-hearted style continues to enchant audiences everywhere.

Lord Inchquin

Arr. Jonathan Adams

CD#1
Track#1
⑤ = G
⑥ = D

D.S. al Coda   Coda

7

Muriel Anderson

Muriel Anderson was raised in a musical family in Downers Grove, Illinois. Her mother taught piano and her grandfather had played saxophone in John Philip Sousa's band. Muriel fell in love with the guitar at age ten and learned every style available to her, culminating in classical guitar study at DePaul University. She went on to study with classical virtuoso Christopher Parkening and with Nashville legend Chet Atkins. In 1989 Muriel won the National Fingerpicking Guitar Championship.

Muriel Anderson has released several CDs: *Heartstrings, Arioso From Paris, Hometown Live, A Little Christmas Gift* (CGD Music) with French guitarist Jean-Felix Lalanne and *Le Duet* (Rarefied Records). Muriel's *Heartstrings* cassette accompanied astronauts into orbit on a space shuttle mission, traveling some 2.5 million miles.

She has released an instructional video with Homespun Tapes—*The Techniques and Arrangements of Muriel Anderson*, and several books, including *Building Guitar Arrangements from the Ground Up, All Chords in All Positions* and *Muriel Anderson Hometown Live* (MB95664BCD). Muriel writes for various guitar magazines and teaches guitar at Belmont University in Nashville.

She originated and hosts "Muriel Anderson's All Star Guitar Night" and has performed at Orchestra Hall in Chicago, the Ryman Auditorium and the Grand Ole Opry in Nashville, Tennessee, and the Olympia Theater in Paris.

RosaLee

Muriel Anderson

⑥ - D

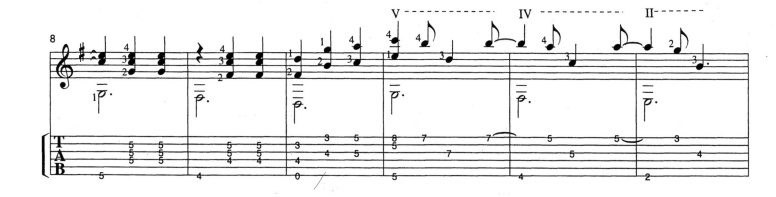

11

Seth Austen

Seth Austen is a virtuoso acoustic fingerstyle guitarist, composer and multi-instrumentalist, who plays in diverse styles including Appalachian, Celtic, bottleneck, Klezmer and jazz. Seth has five solo recordings, most recently *Metamorphosis* and *Desert Winds*, along with three previous releases on Kicking Mule Records; he is a featured artist on two Shanachie anthologies-*The Music Of O'Carolan* and *Silently the Snow Falls*. Seth has also produced, engineered and played on over two dozen recordings by other artists, three of which have won Indie Awards from the National Association of Independent Record Producers (NAIRD).

Seth has composed music for documentaries and radio programs. In 1981, he was a triple winner at The National Flatpicking Championships, Winfield, Kansas, in fingerstyle guitar, mandolin and fretted dulcimer. Seth has been on the faculty of the National Guitar Summer Workshop in New Milford, Connecticut since 1984 and has been a guest artist at numerous festivals, concert stages and seminars throughout the U.S.

Seth's two solo collections, *Bottlenecking Blues & Beyond* (MB97823BCD) and *Fingerstyle Guitar Collection* (MB98141BCD), are published by Mel Bay Publications.

Global Village

"Global Village" is composed using a scale frequently found in Klezmer, flamenco and middle eastern music; D, Eb, F#, G, A, Bb, C, D (1, 2b, 3, 4, 5, 6b, 7b). This mode is built on the fifth degree of the harmonic minor scale, and is sometimes called Ahava Rhaba or freygish.

"Global Village" is in DADGAD, a popular tuning among fingerstyle and Celtic guitarists. Because of the lack of major or minor thirds in the open strings, this tuning is quite versatile for other styles of music as well. DADGAD lends itself to the use of cross-string playing, and I use this technique extensively in this piece. Make sure to hold down fretted notes wile playing other fretted or open notes on adjacent strings. This maximizes the natural resonance of your guitar for a full, rich sound.

"Global Village" begins with a free-form statement of the melodic theme. I then play the piece in 3/4 time, using a hora rhythm which has strong accents on the first and third beats, a different emphasis than what you'd find in a waltz. In the B sections, and also in the third time through the A section, I play a variation expanding the three beat bass pattern across two measures instead of one. For the last two times through the piece, I play the same melodic theme, altered to the time signature of 7/8, a rhythm often used in traditional Greek and Balkan music. This rhythm is counted 3+2+2.

Global Village

Seth Austen

DADGAD

D.R. Auten

D.R. Auten is a recording artist on DRAMA records. Two pieces on his second album were picked up by the Narada record label and went to number 18 in *Billboard* in 1996. His second album was also picked as best album of the month in *Guitar Player Magazine*. D.R. was selected as one of the *New Generation* of guitar players featured in *Acoustic Guitar Magazine* and a five-page special interview was published in *Fingerstyle Guitar Magazine*. D.R. has performed widely in Europe to great acclaim, and enjoys a strong following internationally as well as in the U.S. Since 1995, he has been a featured performer at the Chet Atkins Appreciation Society Convention held in Nashville each July.

D.R. is also an accomplished luthier who has designed and built both electric and acoustic instruments. He has worked for the prestigious Gibson Custom Shop and was one of the original luthiers with the Taylor Guitar Company when it was founded in 1974. His unique and readily identifiable sound—a cross between Chet Atkins, Vince Gill, and James Burton—features hot instrumentals, a strong tenor voice, and clever tune and lyric writing. His music appeals to fans of various styles including country, jazz, folk, bluegrass, world music, new age, and blues. Since its initial publication in this collection, "If I Only Had Wings" was featured in the MGM film *"Heart Breakers"* (March 2001).

If I Only Had Wings

Tuning: DADGAD
Tune down one whole step to match recording

By D.R. Auten

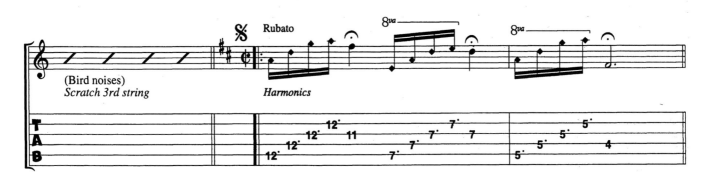

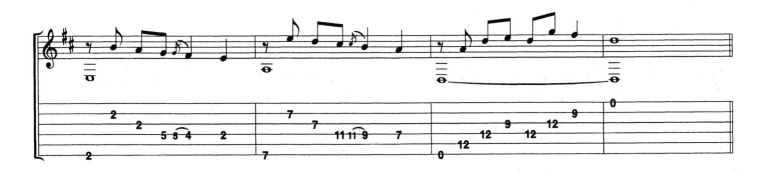

Freely

D.S. al Coda

⊕ Coda

Harmonics

Drum sounds on guitar body

Drum sounds continue

Douglas Back

Douglas Back has earned recognition for his specialization in 19th century American guitar literature. He has presented lecture-recitals and concerts of this music to a variety of audiences nationwide, including the Guitar Foundation of America's 1995 and 1996 International Festivals, Alabama State University, Middle Tennessee State University, and the St. Louis Conservatory of Music. He has published many articles in *Soundboard* and *Guitar Review* and has had two anthologies of music published by Mel Bay Publications.

Mr. Back was the recipient of a National Endowment for the Arts Recording Grant in 1993 and was the first guitarist to record the works of American guitar pioneers William Foden and Justin Holland. He has performed throughout much of the United States and toured Australia in 1994 and the Philippines and Hawaii in 1996. His interviews and performances have been heard on National Public Radio's *All Things Considered*, National Australian Radio, and National Australian Television.

Mr. Back studied at the St. Louis Conservatory of Music, the University of Missouri-St. Louis, and Florida State University. As a student, he won top prize in the George C. Krick Memorial Guitar Competition. His teachers have included Bruce Holzman, Alan Rosenkoetter and Rodney Stucky. Mr. Back resides in Montgomery, Alabama where he directs the guitar programs at Baldwin Arts Magnet School and Troy State University. He is a performing artist in the Alabama State Council on the Arts Touring and Presenting Program.

Breath of Spring

A.J. Weidt
Arr. by Douglas Back

Used by Permission

29

Duck Baker

Duck Baker was born Richard R. Baker IV in Washington, D.C. in 1949 and grew up in Richmond, Virginia. His teenage years were devoted to playing in rock and blues bands before becoming interested in fingerpicking in local coffeehouses. Ragtime pianist Buck Evans was a major influence on Baker's developing interests, which by the time he moved to San Francisco in 1973 included rags, blues, old-time country, cajun, bluegrass and New Orleans jazz. This variety inspired the title of his first solo record, *There's Something for Everyone in America*, released by Kicking Mule Records in 1976.

During the next four years, Baker recorded four more solo records, including one devoted to swing, one to modern jazz and one to Irish and Scottish tunes, and appeared on nine others. He also wrote a book of fiddle tune arrangements and toured incessantly throughout America, Canada, Europe, and Australia. He changed addresses almost as constantly, finally winding up in Europe for most of the '80's. He returned to San Francisco in 1987 and finally to Virginia in 1991. Most of his recent solo recordings have featured his own compositions, an aspect of his work that has drawn particular praise from other guitarists.

If Baker's insistence on studying and performing so many facets of folk and related musics, from medieval European carols to avant-garde jazz, have made him somewhat difficult for the press to categorize, he certainly has earned the respect of his peers. A check list of musicians with whom he has been associated professionally (in performance or on records) would include bluesmen Charlie Musselwhite and Jerry Ricks, bluegrassers Tim O'Brien and Dan Crary, traditionalists Ali Anderson and Brian MacNeil, new music icon John Zorn, rock legend J.J. Cale, and jug band king Jim Kweskin. His fingerpicking peers are on records as saying:

"Duck Baker is a true genius of the guitar." —*Stefan Grossman*

"Duck has discovered a way to write which is purely and originally beautiful. I think he sets a standard we all can aspire to." —*Leo Kottke*

"I suspect that Duck's compositions will make a significant contribution to the [written] repertoire of the guitar, but until then, the music makes fantastic listening." —*John Renbourn*

Duck's Mel Bay books include: *Classic American Folk Blues Themes* (MB95068), *Complete Gospel Guitar Book* (MB96321), *The Guitar of Duck Baker/Fingerstyle Jazz Compositions* (MB96990BCD), and the new *Duck Baker Collection of Scottish, Irish, and American Fiddle Tunes for Fingerstyle Guitar* (MB98545BCD)

Keep It Under Your Heart

GUITAR TUNING: D - A - D - G - B - E

Duck Baker

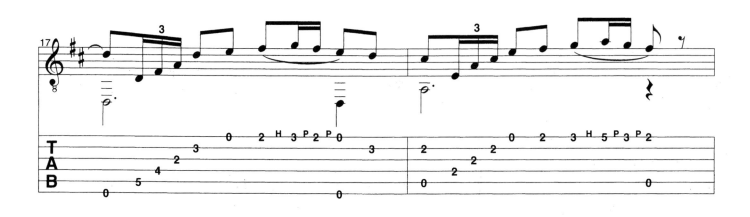

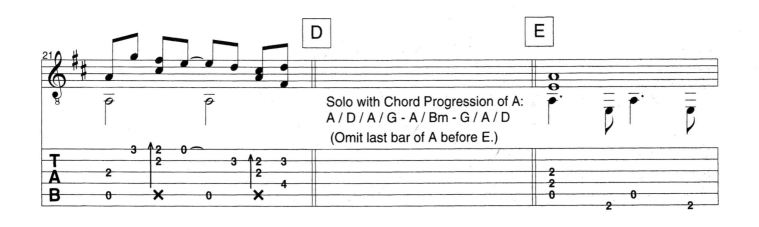

Solo with Chord Progression of A:
A / D / A / G - A / Bm - G / A / D
(Omit last bar of A before E.)

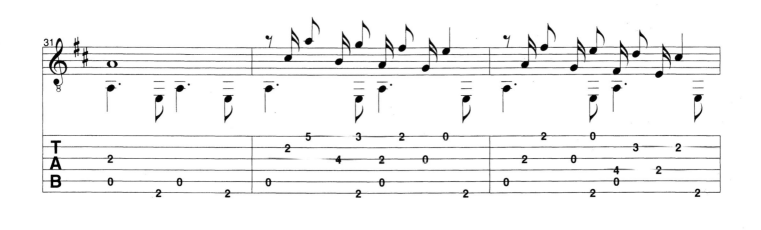

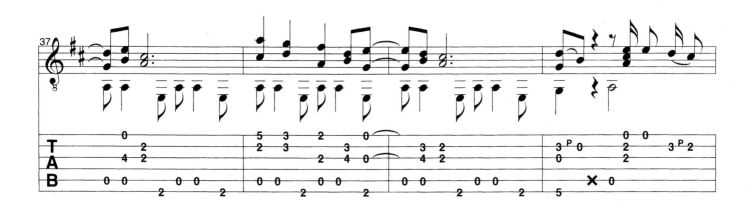

Steve Baughman

Steve Baughman spent his childhood in the Malaysian city of Kuala Lumpur. The sixties were "in" and folk music was big, even in Southeast Asia. Like many kids of that era, he fell in love with the guitar. One day while rummaging through the angklung section of a part-music, part-bicycle shop near a Chinese fruit market, he found a dusty, probably pirated copy of Mel Bay's classic guitar method book. With that book he began the most enriching journey of his life.

Steve Baughman is a pioneer of Celtic and Appalachian fingerstyle guitar. The various right hand techniques he has developed have enabled guitarists around the world to play up-tempo fiddle tunes with ease and fluidity. In this anthology he demonstrates how one such technique, a modified form of old-timey banjo frailing, can be used to play a fast melody effortlessly.

Steve appears on several videos, books and CDs with Celtic guitar greats such as Pierre Bensusan and Martin Simpson. His debut solo album, *A Drop of the Pure*, has been hailed as a cult classic in the world of Celtic fingerstyle guitar.

Steve's solo work can be viewed on the Mel Bay video *Celtic Fingerstyle Guitar Solos* (MB97259VX). His Mel Bay books include *Celtic Fingerstyle Guitar Solos* (MB97259BCD) and *Celtic Guitar Method/Drop of the Pure* (MB96700BCD), *An Open Tunings Christmas for Guitar*, and *Frailing the Guitar*.

Hickory Jack

Tuning: EABEAB
Capo 3rd fret

Traditional, arranged by Steve Baughman

* Middle Finger Thwack

* Percussive Palm Slap

Used by Permission

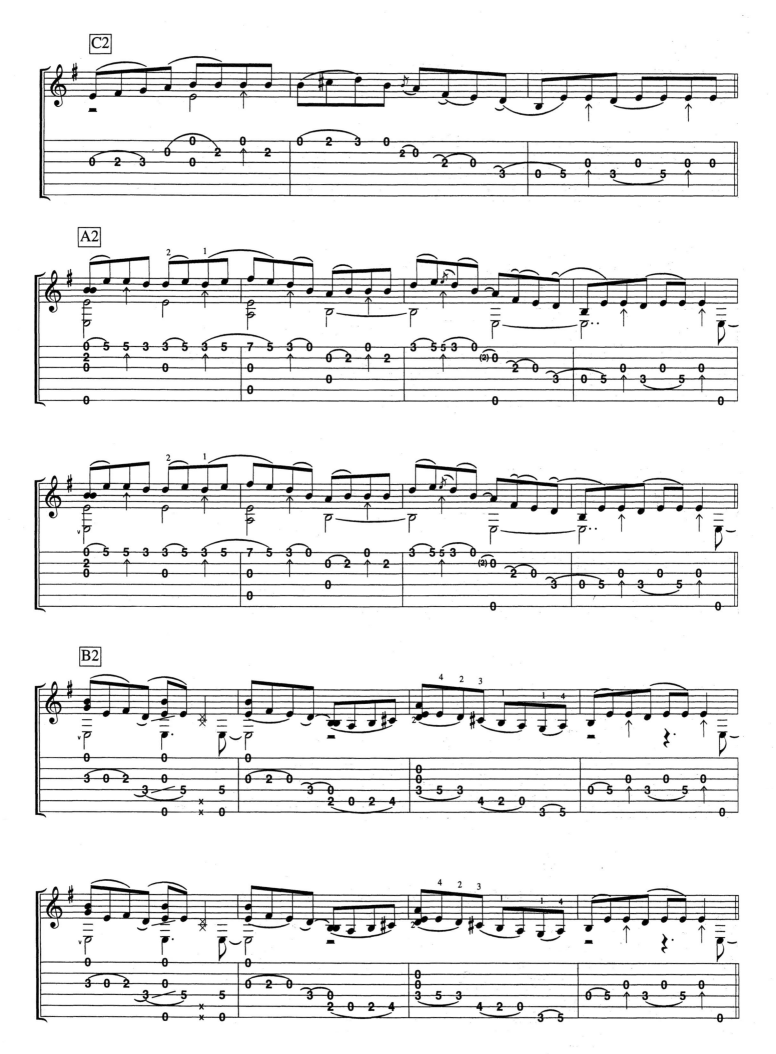

39

William Bay

William Bay is president of Mel Bay Publications, Inc. An accomplished trumpet player and a fine guitarist, he has performed in a wide variety of professional musical settings. Mr. Bay received his undergraduate degree from Washington University in St. Louis and his master's degree from the University of Missouri/Columbia. He has written more than 100 books dealing with a wide assortment of musical topics, instruments, and proficiency levels, with sales in the millions.

Lazy Tuesday

WB

Fingerstyle
Slowly

Fine

D.C. al Fine

Misty Night

* If the fingering is too difficult here, use this phrasing:

Pierre Bensusan

Since bursting on the scene in the mid '70s, Pierre Bensusan's name has become synonymous with contemporary acoustic guitar genius. Throughout his performances and recordings, he has confirmed his place as an acoustic visionary who combined sensibility with shadings of ethereal jazz, folk, pop, ethnic and classical styles, long before the term "world music" was invented. His playing has graced the recordings of many other artists and he has become a legend in his own right at a relatively young age.

Born in 1957 in French Algeria and self-taught as a musician, Pierre first appeared at the Montreux Festival in Switzerland in 1976, where he won the Grand Prix du Disque for his debut album. Manny Greenhill, who manages Joan Baez, Doc Watson and Taj Mahal, invited him to play in the U.S. in 1979 when Rounder Records licensed his recordings. After hundreds of concerts worldwide, numerous recordings and various associations, Pierre was signed to CBS-Masterworks where he released the album *Spices.* In reviewing the album, the *Los Angeles Times* wrote, "[Bensusan is] one of the most admired and copied guitarists of the last 20 years," and artist Leo Kottke once referred to him as "a treasure" (*Acoustic Guitar Magazine*). "A real inspiration" said Suzanne Vega. "This musician is fantastic, he completely blew me away!" said David Crosby after a show in Santa Monica. "The Claude Monet of the guitar" (*Elderly Instruments*). "They haven't invented words to describe Pierre Bensusan or his music. He's unique and original" (*The Oakland Tribune*). He also uses his voice in a truly original way and sings many songs with lyrics written by his wife, Doatea.

As of this writing, even with a very busy touring agenda, Pierre Bensusan has released seven albums, two guitar books, and several videos. He teaches guitar master classes and seminars, and founded his own residential guitar school, where amateur and professional guitar players come from around the world to study with him.

Pierre tours as a solo act and also in duet with Didier Malherby, a founding member of Gong. They released their first duet album, *Live au New Morning,* in 1997 and tour regularly in France and the U.K.

Wu Wei

To Théophile Bensusan

DADGAD (Capo 2)

Larghetto (♩ ±65) Aero

48

Larry Bolles

Larry Bolles grew up playing a variety of instruments. He began teaching himself guitar by copying recordings of acoustic players such as Leo Kottke. "John Renbourn and Baden Powell were major influences for me. They have found ways to combine their love for diverse styles of guitar playing in highly original compositions." Bolles went on to study classical and jazz guitar and was head of classical guitar studies at Webster University for ten years. Larry now divides his time between teaching for St. Louis University, the Musical Arts Academy of Webster Groves, performing, and composing music in a variety of styles. He has a special interest in writing pieces to help fill in the gaps in the classical and popular guitar teaching repertoire.

Prelude & Allegro is basically a daily warm up piece. The first section can be played by beginning students at a moderate tempo. More experienced players should play the repeat and the whole second section at a rapid tempo. The intro section is ideal at a slow tempo to use as a vehicle for refining your right hand technique. Three issues of importance: 1) Your nails should be shaped to offer very little resistance to the string; consult a good teacher or method book. 2) be sure that the bare knuckle (where your finger meets your hand) is centered above the string it is playing so it can pluck from the base without hitting the adjoining string. 3) Cultivating each finger's "firing" at exactly the right time so that the arpeggio is perfectly even. Once you can play the piece evenly and relaxed at a slow tempo, increase your speed to a point where the movement of your right hand becomes a reflex action. You will find by doing so that you can break any imagined speed barrier.

Prelude & Allegro

Larry Bolles

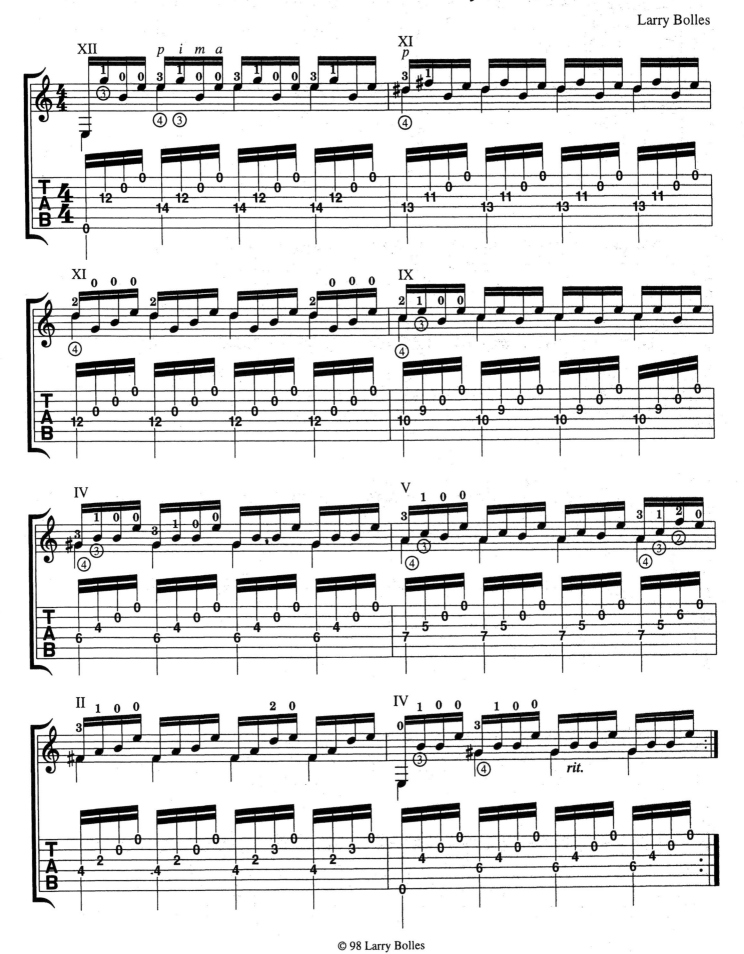

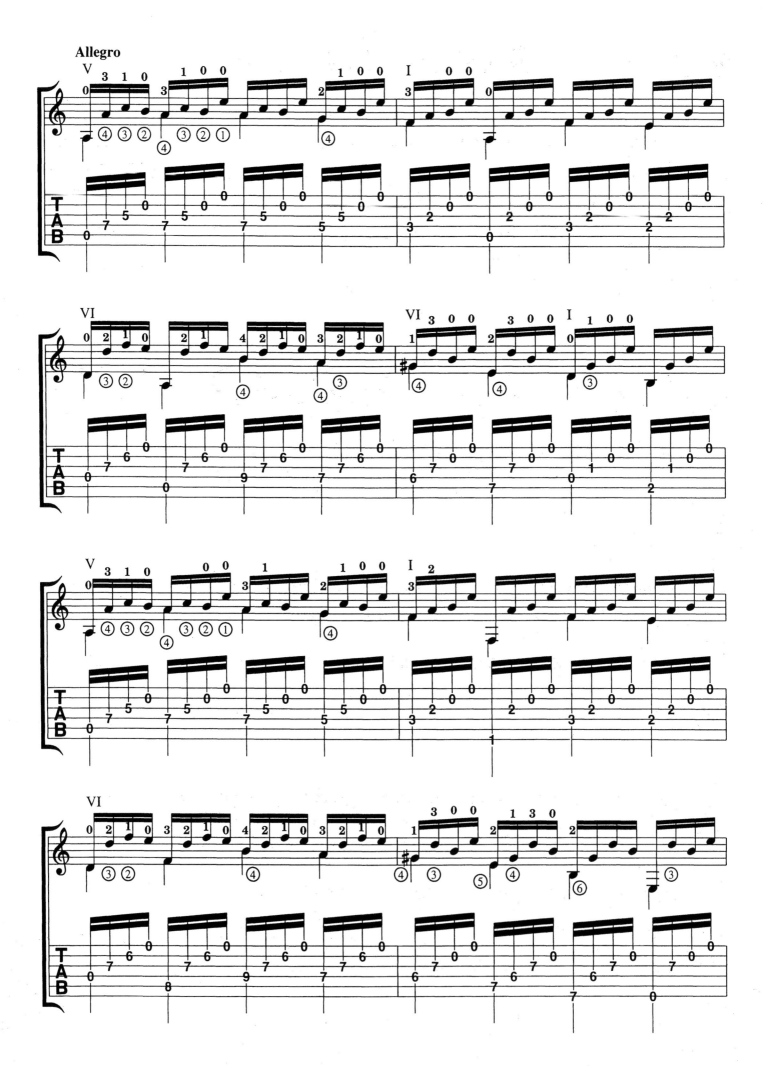

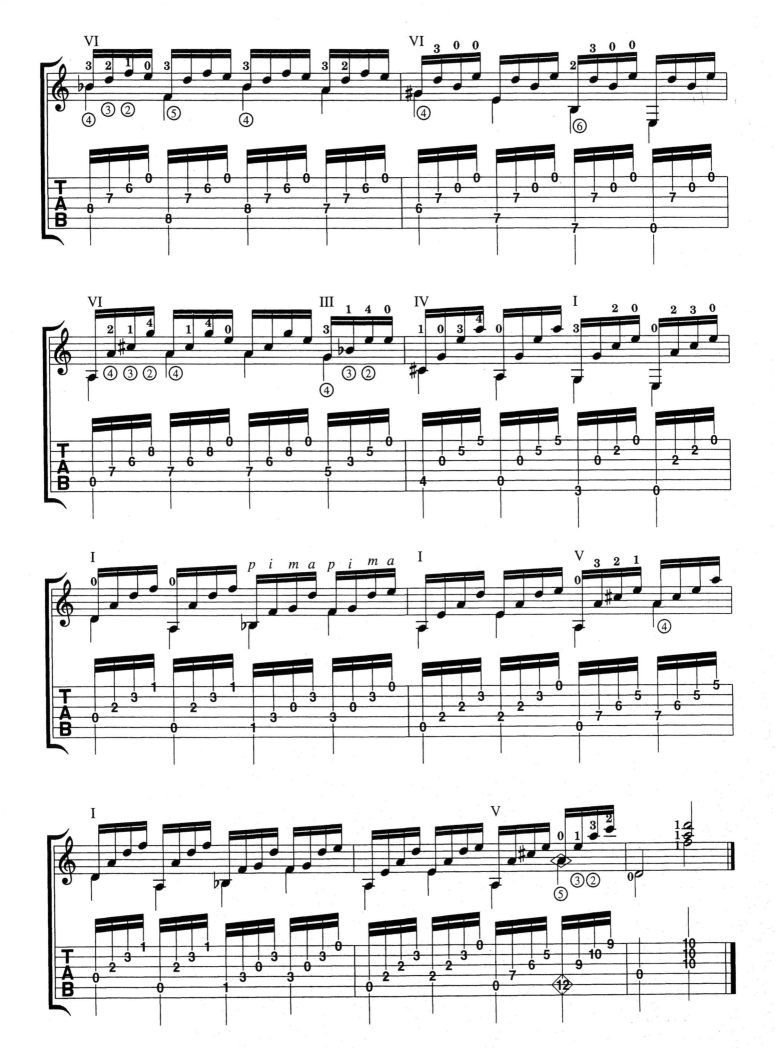

This page has been
left blank to avoid
awkward page turns

Bill Brennan

Bill Brennan began playing guitar when he was ten years of age, and has been a professional guitarist since 1970.

In the sixties, he played in local rock/pop bands, folk clubs, and jazz ensembles. In the years since then, he has played in various musical productions, and has performed solo jazz, classical, blues and traditional guitar.

Bill has been a guitar teacher since the late sixties and now teaches at local schools, colleges and the University of Northumbria in Newcastle upon Tyne.

Irish, Scottish and Border Melodies for Flatpicking Guitar (MB95200BCD), was published by Mel Bay Publications in 1994, and another book, *Irish and Scottish Airs and Ballads for Fingerstyle Guitar* (MB95739BCD), was released in 2001.

By tapping the rich vein of local folk music, and adapting it for his books, Bill has combined his passion for guitar with his deep appreciation of the traditional music of Ireland, Scotland and his own Border Country.

He is married with one daughter and lives in the North East of England. Bill has lived all his life in the town of Prudhoe, in the County of Northumberland.

–Yvonne Brennan

Fay's Hornpipe

This is a hornpipe from the Northumbrian Piper's Tunebook although it's origins could be Irish.

Fay's Hornpipe

Bill Brennan

Used by Permission

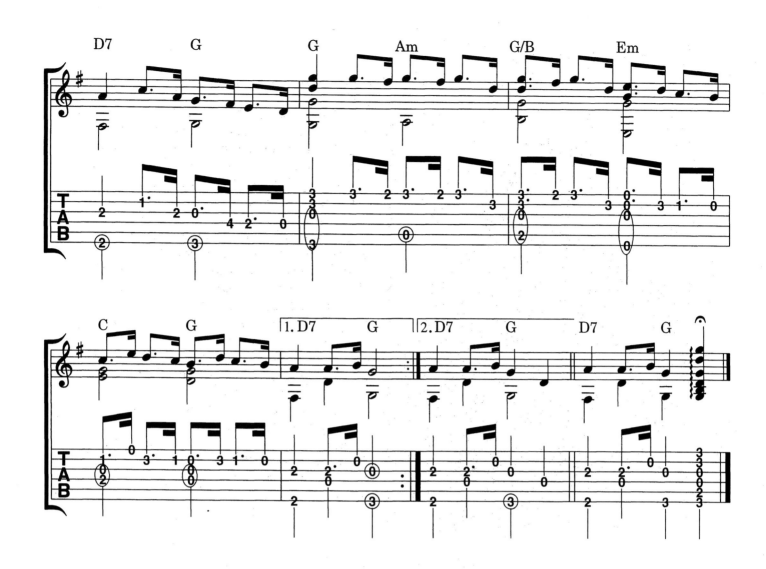

Thom Bresh

Welcome to my music. I'd like to point out that *Hangin' With the Girls I Know* is written as I play it. While the fingerings are the most natural for me, they are by no means the only way to play this piece. It is my hope that you will use what is printed on the page as a guideline for what you might develop on your own. I continue to be amazed by the thinking processes of other musicians who have played their versions of my songs for me. Pat Kirtley plays a great version of *Sidewalks of Bourdeaux.* I wish I had thought of some of the chords he's put in that song! Another friend, Wayne Johnson, is a jazz player who doesn't know anything about throwing his thumb around the neck like a lot of us thumbpickers do. He plays *Hangin' With the Girls I Know* according to his jazz ear, and it's totally different than anything I've ever played. So have fun with the music and just have at it. Maybe something that I've played will spark something in your own musical imagination and lead you into songs of your own.

Hangin' with the Girls I Know

This is one of many songs that I've written at campgrounds. I was sitting on a picnic table, playing around with a bit of a melody, and it lay on the guitar really well. It all just felt really good. The bridge was inspired by a Les Paul album, one that featured his multiple guitar tracks. With that sound in mind, I pulled four strings at once and got that "Les Paul" kind of sound.

As for the title, I played it for my friend Bill Flannery, who produces television shows and that sort of thing, and he said, "Every time you play that, I want to go 'hangin' with the girls I know.' We ought to shoot a video with a whole lot of babes in it." I laughed, and that was the last we spoke of it. The name stuck.

I play this song in just about every concert now. In fact, I usually open with it, because it's easy to get into a lot of different things with it. Also, it's a really good song for testing the sound system as I go on stage. It gives me a chance to find out as I'm walking around the stage where things are feeding back, what I can and can't hear. Aside from all of that, it's just one of my favorite songs to play.

Hangin' with the Girls I Know

Standard Tuning

Thom Bresh

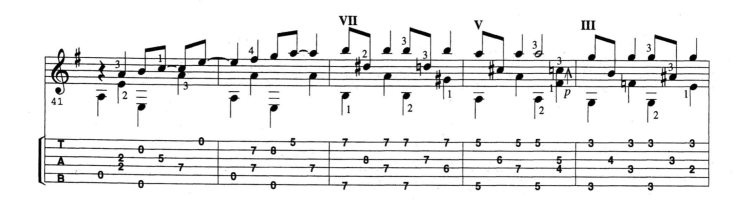

Ben Bolt

Ben Bolt is credited with being the first classical guitarist to introduce thousands of new people to the classical style of guitar through videos and books which use a revolutionary format of learning. In the past, guitar students needed to learn to read music at the same time they were learning to play the guitar, which was complicated. Since the publication of Bolt's book/tape packages, beginners are able to play immediately. The tablature, using lines and numbers to show where the notes are, and the recording, which is rhythmically self-explanatory, empower all students to play. Bolt's work has been emulated throughout the publishing world. Because of his vision of making classical guitar accessible to all kinds of musicians, the classic guitar is being experienced by the masses.

Andrés Segovia, the father of modern classic guitar, said, "Ben Bolt is an excellent guitarist with fine tone." Segovia personally paid for a scholarship so that Bolt could continue his studies at the Música en Compostela summer masterclass and music festival, which Segovia had founded. In his zeal to pursue the Segovia technique and interpretive style, Bolt also studied with one of Segovia's most gifted students, Abel Carlevaro.

Several Ben Bolt books have consistently appeared on Mel Bay's best seller list. His video *Anyone Can Play the Classic Guitar* has become a standard reference for college students on the fundamentals of classical technique. He also appears in Mel Bay's videos of the *Modern Guitar Method*, a huge commercial success selling in the millions of copies.

Bolt divides his time between publishing, performing with orchestras, and teaching at the college level. He believes anyone can play the guitar well, provided they have three ingredients: a good instrument, a knowledgeable teacher, and music that holds the student's interest.

Bolt's work is distributed internationally and has been featured at the annual NAMM show (National Association of Music Merchants) in California, as well as the international music fair in Frankfurt, Germany.

Scarborough Fair

Arranged by Ben Bolt

Freely (ad lib.)

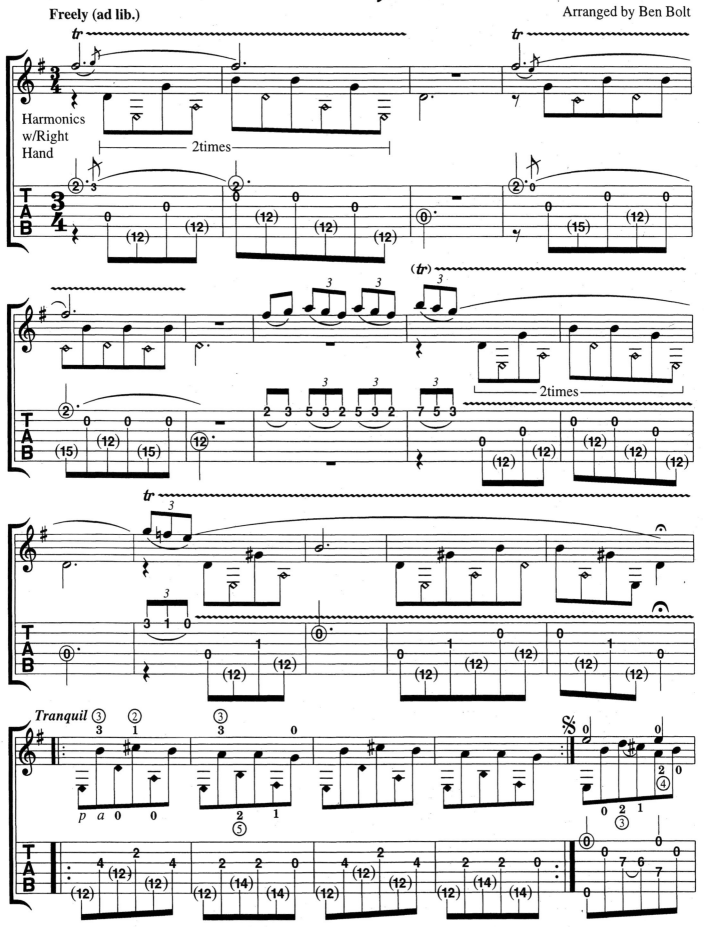

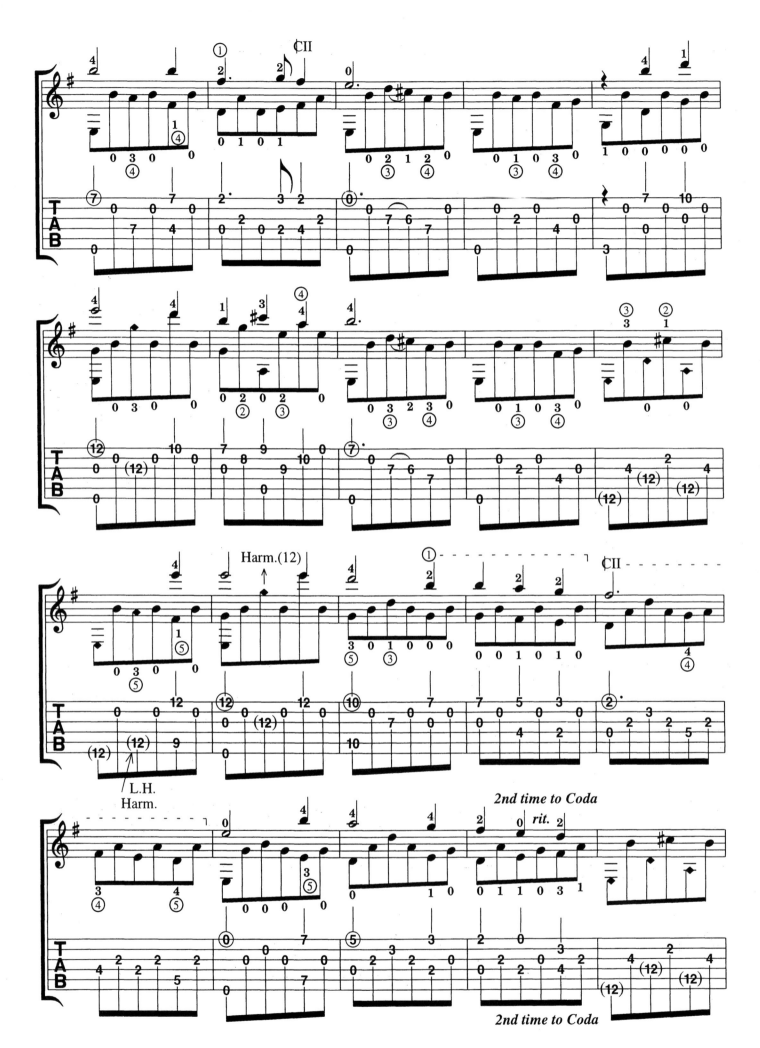

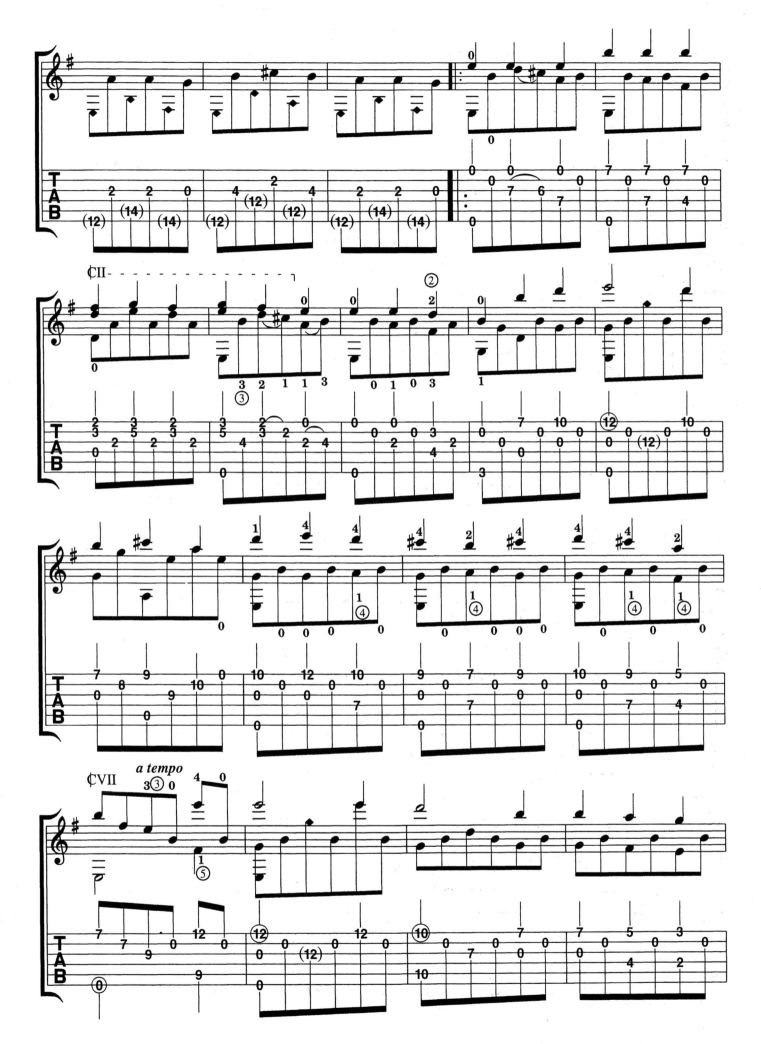

67

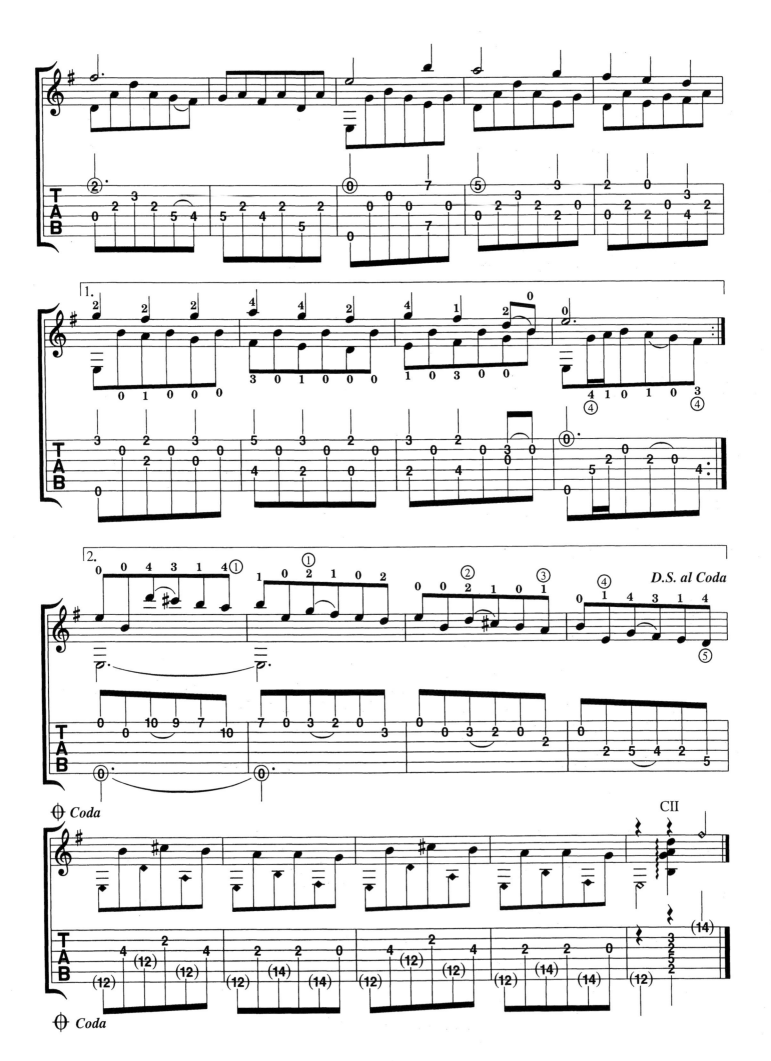

Rolly Brown

In more than three decades of guitar playing, Rolly Brown has covered a lot of territory. Geographically, that territory includes gigs extending from the Philadelphia Folk Festival to the Tasmanian Folk Festival. Musically, the territory is even more diverse. Beginning as a folk guitarist, Brown moved on to become an acclaimed master of ragtime, country blues, electric blues, country, classic rock, bluegrass, & jazz styles. Proficient on acoustic and electric guitars, his mission has been to integrate many styles while retaining a very singular style.

"For me," Brown says, "the battle has been to absorb the work of my favorite guitarists; Rev. Gary Davis, George Van Eps, Mark Knopfler, Blind Blake, Lenny Breau, Joseph Spence, Pierre Bensusan, and others without sacrificing my own personal style, which listeners have described as fluid and melodic."

This quest has included long periods of time during which Brown has settled into particular genres: singer-songwriter periods', a jazz standard era, a ragtime blues cycle, a folk fingerpicker epoch, and most recently, a bluegrass flatpicking period. Later, his performances began to include many of these elements: some singing, some instrumentals, something old, and something new. Recent concerts have featured this eclecticism in the fingerstyle realm along with some serious flatpicking which has grown out of Rolly's collaboration and friendship with Winfield Flatpicking Champ, Mark Cosgrove.

To date, Rolly has released two CDs of solo fingerstyle guitar on his Aussie Dog label. The first, *No Need for Words* (1992), is a series of meditative improvisations on the guitar. The second, *Max's Ramble* (1997), is a collection of Rolly's favorite tunes and compositions, highlighting the more virtuosic side of his playing.

Along the way, Brown has been a solo performer, a teacher (his students have included Marcy Marxer, Freyda Epstein, Magpie, Priscilla Herdman, Jay Ansill, and Eric Lugosch), a radio producer and announcer, a studio player, a band member, and a sideman. When he puts down the guitar, he teaches Chinese martial arts and practices and teaches traditional Chinese acupuncture. " A person can't completely master even one of these arts. I'm never bored."

Chapel Road

Rolly Brown

6th = D

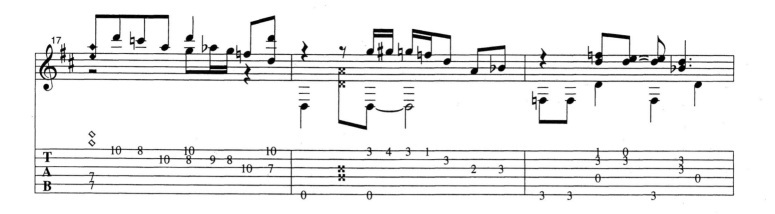
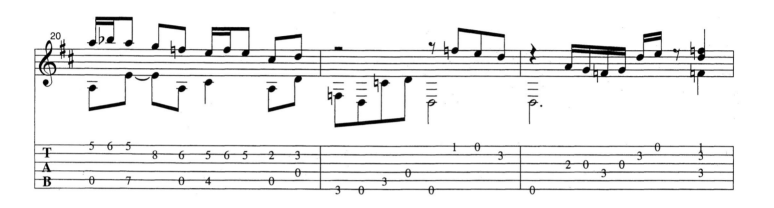
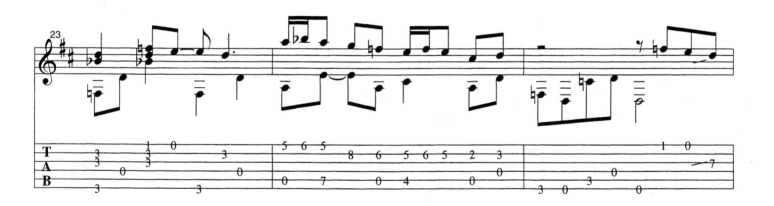
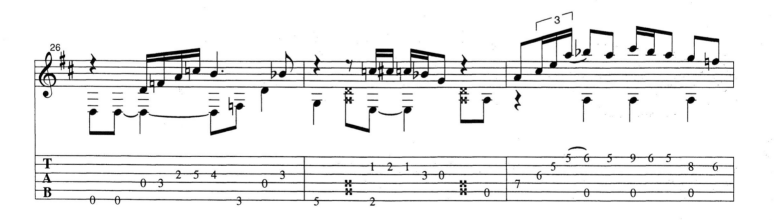

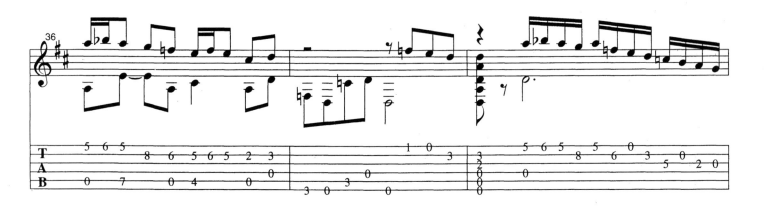

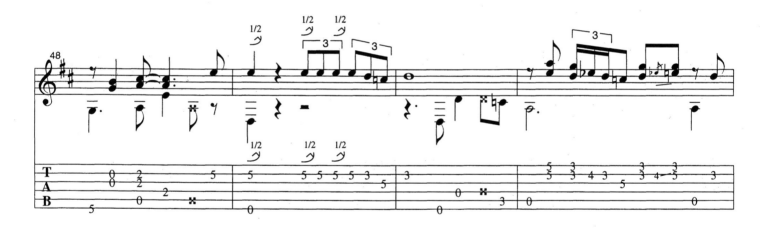

D.S. al Coda

Coda ⊕

Robin Bullock

Robin Bullock is a Maryland-based multi-instrumentalist whose recordings and performances are redefining the connection between Celtic and North American folk music traditions. His mastery of acoustic guitar, mandolin, fiddle and the rare and beautiful cittern has won him many competitions and earned praise from such publications as *Acoustic Guitar, Classical Guitar, Dirty Linen* and *Sing Out!* He has been a member of the acoustic trio Helicon since its formation in 1987, and with them has recorded three CDs and toured widely throughout North America and Europe. He also collaborates frequently with hammered dulcimer artists Walt Michael and Maggie Sansone, singer Lisa Moscatiello, and dance ensemble Footworks. He is highly sought after as an instructor, having taught privately in the Baltimore area since 1987 and led festival workshops from coast to coast; Robin is on the faculties of the Swannanoa Gathering at Warren Wilson College, Asheville, North Carolina, and Common Ground at Western Maryland College, in Westminster, Maryland. Presently he is at work on a third solo CD and a full-length guitar instruction book.

Lost Hollow Lament

Slow and wistful

Robin Bullock

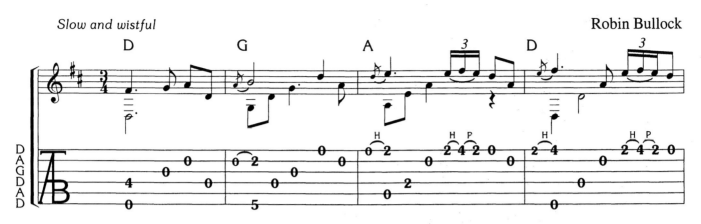

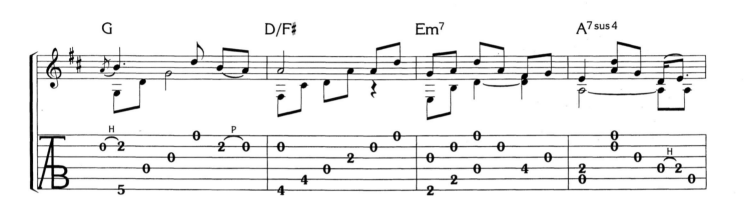

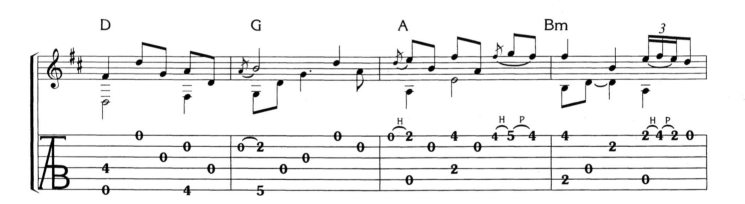

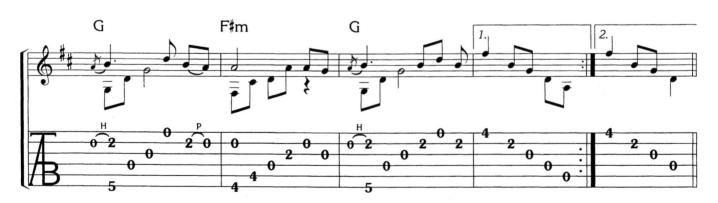

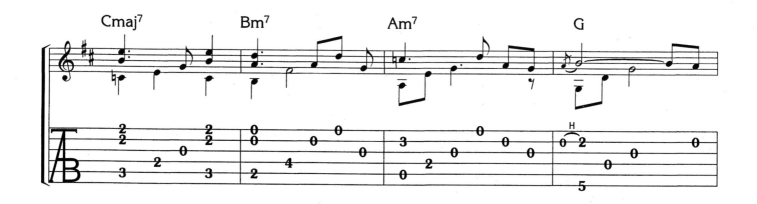

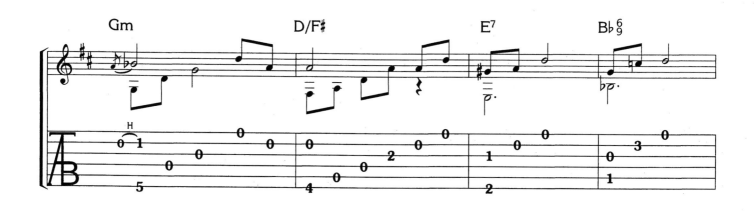

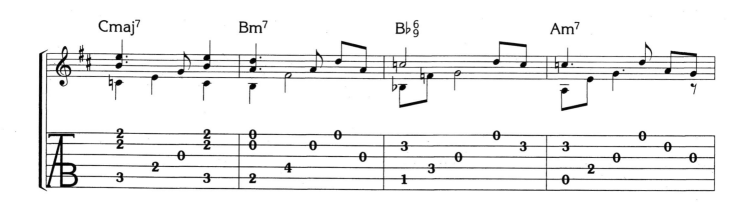

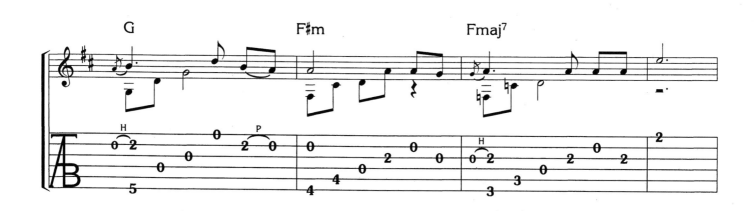

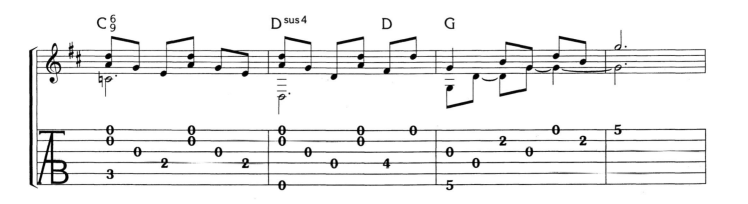

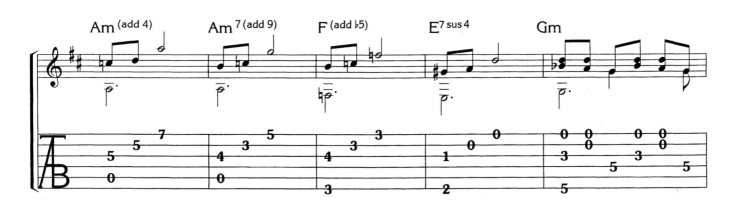

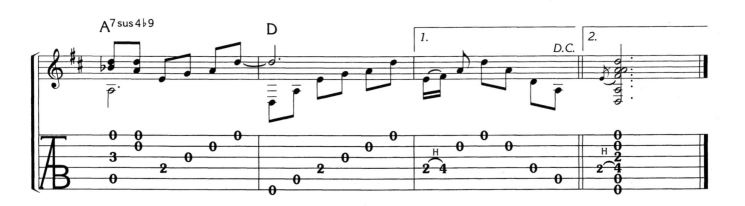

Jonathan Burchfield

As a youngster, Jonathan would watch his father play fingerstyle guitar, then try to emulate what he saw. "Besides guitar, I remember my dad showing me a few banjo pieces when I was real young, but didn't realize how much that would affect my guitar playing later. Many of the things I play today, whether classical or jazz, have a slight banjo feel to them. One year when I was playing for the Chet Atkins Appreciation Society in Nashville for about three or four hundred guitarists, I ended this classical style piece with a fast, single line run; then, as part of a workshop, I slowed it down for the audience and they immediately recognized it as the familiar banjo run we all used to hear on the Hee Haw theme song. It's amazing how closely related these instruments are."

At age 18, Jonathan left home to travel with a 13 piece group called The Spurrlows. At the time they were the back-up group for country star, Roy Clark. During a typical concert Roy would introduce Jonathan from Happy Valley, Tennessee, then they would break into the old song *Dueling Banjos*. It was during those years that Jonathan learned the most on guitar because of the regular company he kept with Roy and other great players.

At age 21, Jonathan left his life on the road and settled back in with his family. They spent their winters in Bourbonnais, Illinois and summers in their East Tennessee home. He taught guitar for a number of years and worked as a recording musician along with his brothers in several Chicago studios. They began driving back and forth to Nashville, their permanent home.

Jonathan took a job as guitarist and banjo player at Opryland for about 7 years, including the Roy Acuff Theatre, the General Jackson Showboat and the Opryland Hotel. He also helped form a trio called 78 RPM which specialized in old jazz standards of the '30s and '40s. They even dressed the part with old silk ties and outfits from yesteryear.

Jonathan tours full time now with his brother Ben. They travel as a guitar and marimba duo playing churches, cruises and festivals. On occasion they are joined by their brother Mark on bass and his wife, Wanda Vick who is a multi-instrumentalist. Jonathan has recorded several CDs and usually tabs a book to accompany each one. The CD, *Smoky Mountains Precious Memories* received a Dove Nomination in '95. He writes for various guitar publications and conducts workshops on occasion. He has also written books for other players, the most recent being Doyle Dykes.

Clair De Lune

This piece is to be played with a lot of feeling. The timing of the note values are not to be followed too closely, after all it is Impressionistic. For the most part it should be played tenderly, and with a lot of freedom. To achieve that soft, delicate feel in this song, harmonics will be your best friend. Not only do they create a tender mood, they also make it possible to reach notes that normally could only be played on the piano. I treat this almost like a harp in that I roll many of the chords. I've marked a few of the more important rolls but I roll quite a bit more than I indicated on paper. Feel free to do the same.

Measure 1 Anytime you see an (ip) next to the harmonic, touch and pluck the note 12 frets above the fingered note. Your first harmonic in this measure is "E" (5th fret 2nd string). Finger the note at the 5th fret and pick the note 12 frets above (17th fret) with your right hand thumb while simultaneously touching it with your right hand index finger to sound the harmonic. Notice the "E" note will then sound one octave higher.

Also, hold this chord down throughout the measure. The only finger that should move is the 4th on the high "C#". This will allow a very smooth beginning. In this arrangement you should hold chords throughout the measures every chance you get.

Measure 2 In this case, hold your 2nd finger in place ("F" natural on the 3rd string, 10th fret) through the entire measure. Also there is no (ip) here, so play these natural harmonics as you normally would on the 12th fret.

Measure 3 This is a little different fingering than I did on the CD. The first few years of playing this piece I sat holding the guitar classical style. Since then I've been standing throughout my concerts using a shoulder strap. The reason I bring this up is because measure 3 is hard to play in tune while standing unless it's fingered and played in this position. You'll find a close rendition of the original fingering at measure 81.

Measure 7 When you roll the last chord of this measure, playing (piam) will make the notes sound in the right order. It feels awkward at first, but if you practice rolling your hand in that order a few times it will begin to feel more natural.

Measure 42, 43 It's important to keep these two measures barred on the 7th fret the whole time. This will really smooth out the triplets.

Measure 56 Once you're past this measure, your home free. It's probably the toughest stretch especially if you are playing a regular classical without a cut away. It will help to hold the neck up higher and closer to you on this one.

Measure 85 Notice the first two octave harmonics are touched 12 frets above the fingered notes (10th fret). That puts you at the 22nd fret which is practically at the end of the fingerboard. If its past the fingerboard, you'll find the harmonics somewhere in the middle of the sound hole. At first you'll have to search for them, but eventually you will get used to them and probably hit them every time. The measure ends with a natural harmonic played on the 12th fret.

Measure 77 Here is one exception to the harmonic rule. Think of it as 12 frets above the open "D". You will actually be picking the note at the 12 fret, not the 24th. It's really a natural harmonic to be played on the 12, But I put the (ip) there because of the right hand technique used on these two measures.

Measure 101 The key to speed in these measures is to play rather lightly with a very relaxed right hand. These triplets are very effective in this piece because of their harp like nature. I take a lot of liberty in how many triplets to play in these first and second endings. When you feel like you've played the right amount, end the measure and go on.

I hope you enjoy this arrangement. It has been a favorite of mine for many years.

– Jonathan Burchfield

Clair De Lune

Arranged by
JONATHAN BURCHFIELD

CLAUDE DEBUSSY

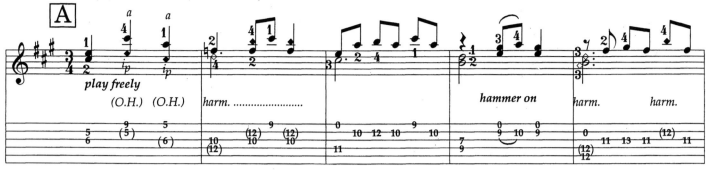

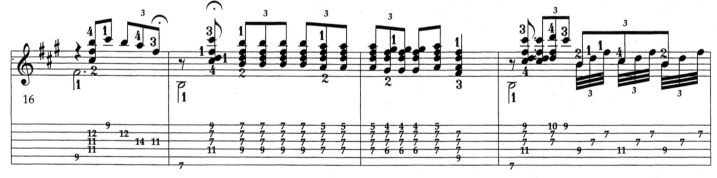

83

Michael Chapdelaine

From Lincoln Center to the Cactus Cafe in Austin, Michael Chapdelaine continues to enchant, dazzle and surprise audiences and critics alike as he redefines the modern acoustic guitar with his amazing technique, "soulful" expressiveness, and versatility as a performer, composer and arranger/producer. His performances, played on both steel string and classical guitars, include musical styles ranging from blues to Bach to country to rhythm n' blues as he wins his audience's hearts with breath-taking technique and the poetic magic of his original musical portraits and landscapes.

In the '80s and '90s Michael proved himself to be one of the world's finest classical guitarists; twice winning the coveted National Endowment for the Arts Solo Recitalist Grant, and taking First Prize in both the Guitar Foundation of America and the Music Teachers National Association guitar competitions. He also won the Silver Medal in Venezuela's VIII Concurso International de Guitarra "Alirio Diaz." He has toured three continents while giving hundreds of performances for Affiliate Artists Inc., and various arts promotion organizations. In 1992 he recorded the *Sonata Romantica* CD, which many critics and connoisseurs of classical guitar consider to be one of the definitive recordings for the instrument. *Acoustic Guitar* magazine wrote "...if I were marooned on a desert island with a limited selection of recordings, this one would be among my choices...I have seldom heard a more beautiful album. Other young guitarists have excellent technique, but few have such style and musicality, and Chapdelaine's beautiful tone is the nearest to Segovia's that I can recall."

In 1994 Michael turned his attention to pop music in arranging, producing and recording Time-Life Music's beautiful *Guitar by Moonlight* collection, which sold 250,000 copies in its first two years in the stores. In 1998, he once again, expanded his musical range and gained instant notoriety and credibility in the "acoustic music" world as a "fingerstyle" guitarist and composer, by winning the National Fingerpicking Championships at Winfield. *Soundboard* called his suite *Red Sand, Homage to the American Indian* "an impressionistic, gently modal work, melancholy, but never depressing, which used parallel fourths, bent notes, glissandi, and other devices to evoke rather than imitate Native American music...an ambitious and original work; Chapdelaine is as formidable a composer as he is a guitarist."

Michael is a Professor of Music and head of guitar studies at the University of New Mexico, and has previously been on the faculties of the University of Colorado at Denver and Metropolitan State University. He has given master classes throughout the U.S. at major universities including University of Miami, Mannes School of Music, the University of Texas, and California State University.

His teachers included the great Spanish maestro Andres Segovia.

A collection of Michael's solos titled *Land of Enchantment: Musical Postcards from New Mexico* (MB98364) will be published and distributed by Mel Bay Publications.

Cowboy Waltz

Michael Chapdelaine

ad libitum lonesome prarieumn

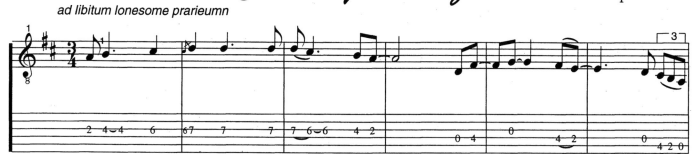

country swing ♩ = 100

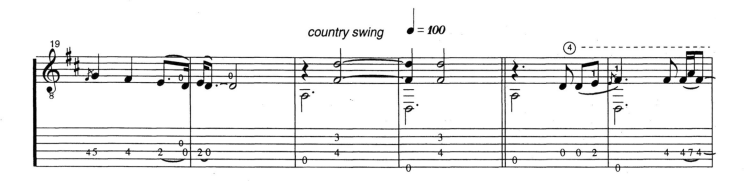

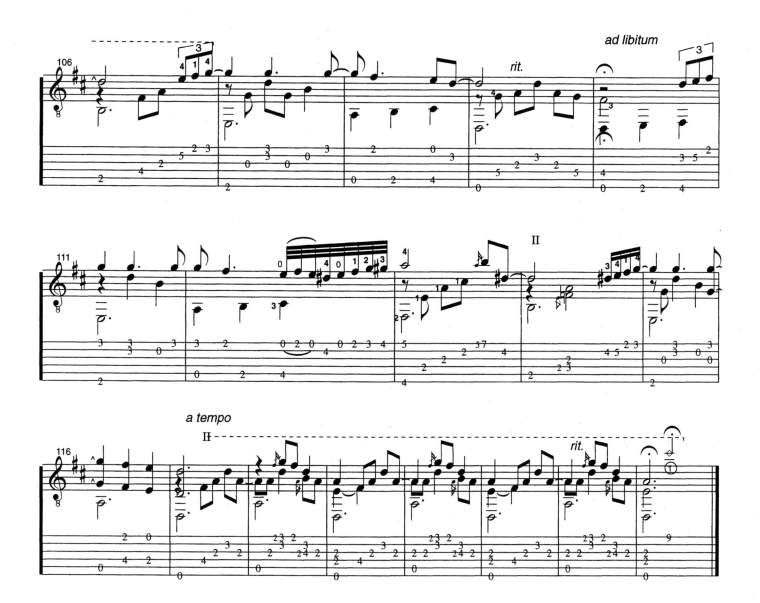

91

Michael Christiansen

Mike Christiansen is a Professor and Director of Guitar Studies in the Music Department at Utah State University where he was presented with the 1994 *Professor of the Year Award*. He has conducted many workshops for guitarists and educators. Mike has played in various ensembles and bands, has written and recorded radio jingles, done back-up work on recordings, and has written and recorded for TV and educational films. In addition to performing as a soloist, Mike is a member of the groups Mirage and The Lightwood Duo.

Remembering Linda

CD #1
Track #19

Michael Christiansen

William Coulter

William Coulter has been recording and performing traditional music in the San Francisco Bay area since 1981. He has been a member of many ensembles including Isle of Skye, Orison, and Gravity Hill. In 1995 he released his first solo recording on the Gourd music label called *Celtic Crossing,* and in 1997 he released a follow-up recording called *Celtic Sessions.* His recordings have been featured on three different *Billboard* Top 10 collections of Celtic music on the Narada Music label, He has also recorded three critically acclaimed CDs of traditional Shaker melodies, *Simple Gifts, Tree of Life,* and *Music on the Mountain,* with cellist Barry Phillips. Since 1994 he has toured the United States, performing at Shaker villages, festivals, and in concert with The Coulter-Phillips Ensemble. In 1998 on the Windham Hill label, he released a CD called *Celtic Requiem* with the Irish singer Mary McLaughlin. William holds a master's degree in guitar performance from the San Francisco Conservatory of Music and a master's degree in enthnomusicology from the University of California.

Bill's solo collection, *Celtic Crossing* (MB96316) is published by Mel Bay Publications.

Mo Ghille Mear

MacDhomnaill

DADGAD
Capo III

guitar acc. to flute / English horn melody

96

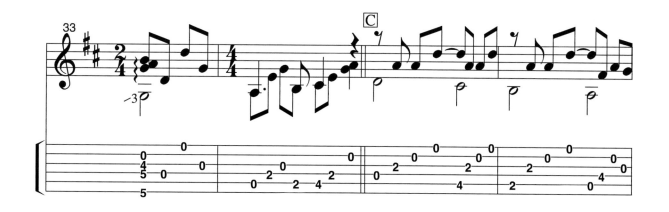

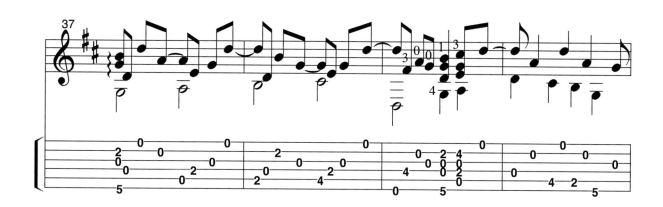

resume guitar solo with cello and piano 2nd time

Marcel Dadi

Marcel Dadi popularized the Chet Atkins style throughout Europe, enhancing it with stylistic and technical advances of his own. He was also instrumental in establishing the Atkins-Dadi Guitar Players Association conference in Issoudun, France where he had performed annually with Chet Atkins and other Nashville associates since 1991. Marcel left a legacy of recordings, concert videos, and meticulous instructional videos based on the Atkins and Travis styled he had mastered. He also produced three volumes of outstanding fingerstyle guitar compositions.

In addition to his many introspective tunes, Marcel unabashedly conveyed his love of family and friends, or paid respectful tribute to musicians who had influenced him by composing a tune in their honor. The tables of contents in his books might typically read: *From Paris with Love, Holidays with Samuel, Lullaby for Stephanie, My Old Friend Pat, Number One Son, Song for Jerry, Song for Chet (also Merle, Doc, and Kathy!), Song for Ma Femme (My Wife), To Mom and Dad, Lovely Gene, Like Father Like Son, and Nou Trois (We Three)*. Marcel Dadi perished in the tragic crash of TWA flight 800 in 1996. He was famous for his easy accessibility to fans. For those who were not fortunate enough to meet him personally, it is still possible to know Marcel as a close friend by playing his music.

Marcel can be seen in the Mel Bay video, *Marcel Dadi & Jean-Felix Lalanne/Olympia 1988* (MB97521VX). His solos are available in *Marcel Dadi, Fingerpicking Guitar Legend* (MB94851BCD). In 2001, Mel Bay Publications released a tribute entitled *Remembering Marcel/ 19 Fingerstyle Guitar Solos Celebrating the Life of Marcel Dadi* (99759BCD).

Song for Chet

Transcribed by
Bill Piburn

Marcel Dadi

Barre with 4

101

105

106

Peppino D'Agostino

Guitarist Peppino D'Agostino immigrated to America in 1985 to pursue his dream as both a composer and performer. Those early days as a struggling street musician (and sometimes house painter and vegetable seller) in San Francisco now seem far behind.

The adventurous guitarist has since released several critically acclaimed albums in the U.S. and Europe. D'Agostino has been praised by the *San Francisco Chronicle* as "a poet...among the best talents around," lauded by *Acoustic Guitar* as "one of the most capable composers among fingerstyle guitarists," applauded by the *San Diego Times* as "potentially a giant of the acoustic guitar," and touted by *Jazziz* as a "phenom in the same league with John Fahey, Leo Kottke, Doc Watson and John Renbourn." A busy touring schedule has whisked him from Carnegie Hall to Wolftrap, and to music venues such as the Vancouver Festival where he's shared the stage with such noted guitarists as Leo Kottke, Doc Watson, Chet Atkins, Laurindo Almeida, Michael Hedges, David Bromberg, David Grisman, John Lee Hooker and Egberto Gismonti.

The Dancer

This beautiful piece is an excellent example of the guitar music of Peppino D'Agostino, who has been praised by both critics and aficionados since the mid-1980s as a virtuosic and original voice on the instrument. The transcription has been edited to conform to the space requirements of this book; a full transcription of The Dancer will be available in the near future in a book of Peppino's music done in collaboration with Peter Finger, to be distributed by Mel Bay.

In the extended rubato introduction, Peppino exhibits a melodic and very romantic approach. One can hear a certain folk quality in his style, but all the notes are clearly played, and the listener is always sure of his musical intent.

Beginning with an arpeggiated F♯ minor chord, the piece immediately surprises by landing on G Major 9. The entire first system is played in 2nd position. Measures 5-7 repeat the initial material with some variation, liquidating into a dynamic figure with a moving bass line. The passages resolves lyrically from D through C♯7 to F♯ major.

Measures 11-18 are an extended variation of the first section. It is interesting to examine the notes in measures 14-17. When looked at purely as melody, they are extremely simple. But with the bass line that Peppino establishes, and the manner of overall execution, the music truly comes alive. A whole tone passage on the dominant C♯7 returns us one final time to F♯ (Major) and a transition, complete with cadenzas, into the section in tempo at measure 28.

The "Dance" section opens with a B minor turnaround, I - VI - ♭VI - V. This passage is never thicker than two notes, but it is played with such authority that it sounds bigger than it is. Great guitarists from Andres Segovia to John Lee Hooker can do this kind of thing, but it takes a lot of personal strength and musical maturity to play a simple melody or pattern and "fill the room."

Most of the piece from this point involves a tremolo pattern and melody played in the bass. This technique is difficult to perfect, but once mastered, it uses the full range of the guitar, and is an effective contrast to the lush chord solo passages that come earlier in the piece.

This 6-page transcription contains exact notes and tab from Peppino D'Agostino's 1998 CD on Acoustic Music Records, [A Glimpse of Times Past.] Although edited, it provides a wealth of insights into the compositional style and guitar techniques of one of this generation's outstanding fingerstyle guitarists. A student can extrapolate from this material and finish transcribing the entire piece, or consult the above-mentioned book.

The Dancer
by Peppino D'Agostino

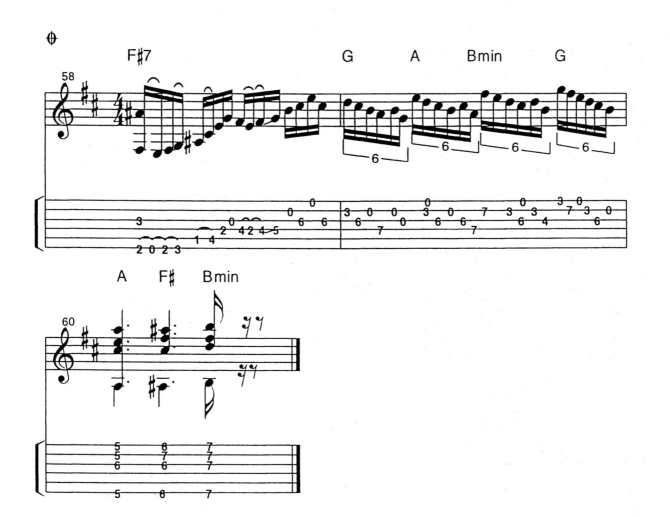

Craig Dobbins

Craig Dobbins lives in Gadsden, Alabama, with his wife Julie, and son Craig Bennett Jr. His books and recordings include *The Guitar Style Of Jerry Reed, Fingerpickin' Guitar Solos, Hymns For Fingerstyle Guitar*, and *Down Home Picking* (MB96933BCD). He has written for such publications as *Acoustic Guitar Magazine, Fingerstyle Guitar Magazine* and *Mister Guitar* (journal of the Chet Atkins Appreciation Society).

Craig also writes and publishes *Acoustic Guitar Workshop*, a quarterly instructional package featuring fingerstyle arrangements in notation and tab, with teaching comments and cassette.

Love Lifted Me

Words by James Rowe

Music by Howard E. Smith

Arranged by Craig B. Dobbins

115

116

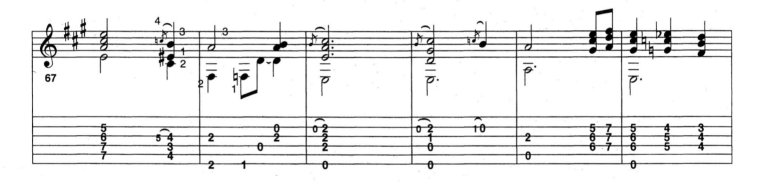

Pat Donohue

Pat Donohue is "a masterful guitarist and talented singer-songwriter of blues, folk and jazz" (*Los Angeles Times*). His talents are displayed weekly in his appearances on public radio's *A Prairie Home Companion*, where his guitar playing, writing and singing are featured regularly.

The 1983 National Finger Picking Guitar Champion, Donohue's style blends blues and folk in a critically acclaimed display of guitar artistry. His original songs have been recorded by Chet Atkins, Suzy Bogguss, Loose Ties and other stellar performers. He has been a featured performer at major music festivals, including the Newport Folk Festival, Telluride Festival, and the Philadelphia Folk Festival, and performs regularly in concerts and clubs around the country.

Donohue has just released his fourth recording, *Backroads*, on Minnesota's Bluesky Records label. A collection of all new original songs, *Backroads* includes musical support from such artists as Chet Atkins, Howard Levy and Butch Thompson. His previous recordings are *Two Hand Band, Life Stories*, and *Big Blind Bluesy*.

Pat Donohue's guitar skills are shared through many instructional venues. His extensive travels for *A Prairie Home Companion* and his solo performance engagements, enable him to conduct in-person group workshops throughout the nation. He participates in teaching camps, most recently this summer at the August Heritage in Elkin, West Virginia, where he taught advanced swing and blues. He also has three videos out on Stefan Grossman's Vestapol series: *Jazz Classics for Finger Style Guitar, Rags to Rock*, and a performance video, *In Concert at the Freight & Salvage*, which not only displays his wide-ranging guitar styles, but also features the warmth and humor he brings to his live performances.

Although he went to college in Milwaukee and lived and performed in Denver for a number of years, Pat Donohue is a life-long resident of St. Paul, Minnesota, where he currently lives with his wife, Susan and daughter, Daisy.

High Society

Transcribed by
Bill Piburn

Pat Donohue

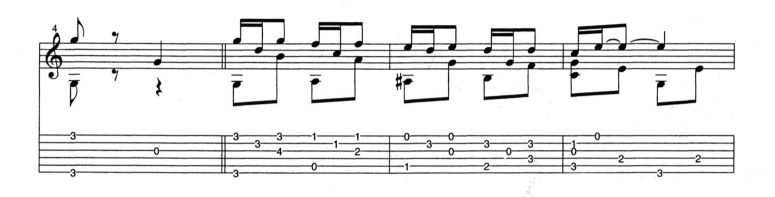

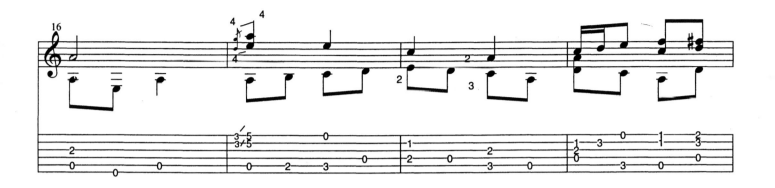

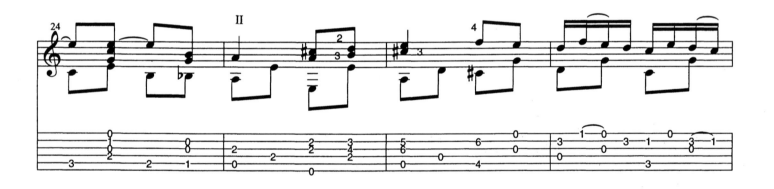

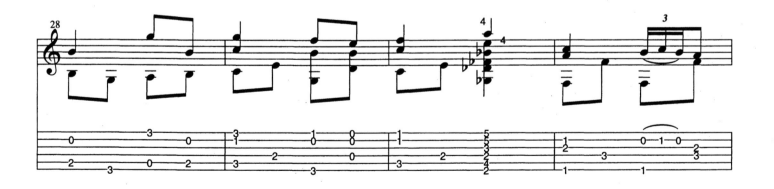

123

Fan with index

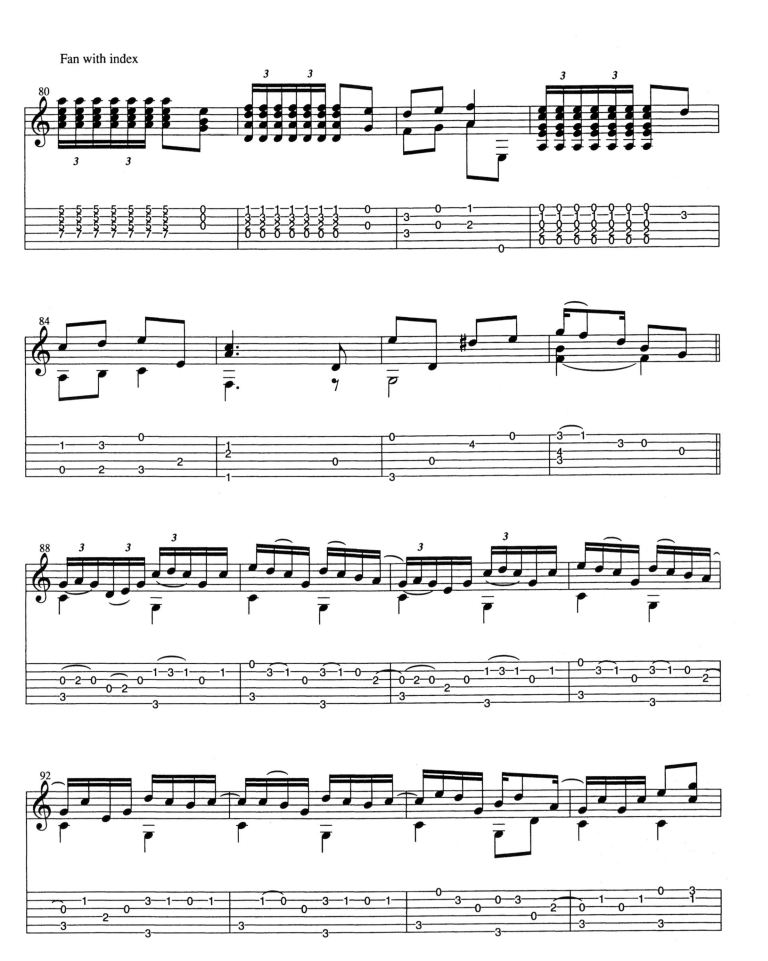

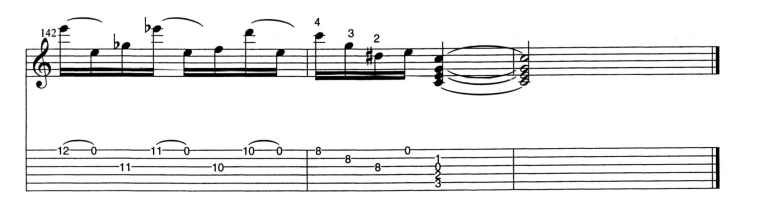

Doyle Dykes

Doyle Dykes is unequivocally one of today's brightest-shining stars within the arena of fingerstyle guitar. In an era where indulgent, new age droning has become passe, Dykes has breathed new life into the form of contemporary acoustic guitar, amalgamating flamenco fire, sparkling balladic harmonies, virtuosic tremolo, molten-hot single-not passages, and southern alternating bass techniques into a form of all-too-rare steel-string ascendancy. But he is not just another in-your-face technician; his compositions teem with aggressive originality, and his takes on standard hymns are enough to convert even the most jaded listener. In a nutshell, Dykes draws deeply from his well of spiritual and musical influences, and pours out fresh water-music that both transfixes our ears and captivates our hearts. But Dykes' ride to relative stardom has not been overnight; though he has recently come to the attention of the wider CD-buying public via his '98 Windham Hill release *Gitarre 2000*, he has been plying his trade for years.

Growing up in Jacksonville, Florida, Dykes was surrounded by a musical family. Receiving his first guitar (a Sears) in his early teens, he immediately went to work, extricating licks from his favorite records. "I listened to a lot of Chet Atkins and Merle Travis," recalls Dykes, "but I couldn't figure out how they were doing what they did. Out of ignorance, I tried to emulate it with a straight pick. Later, a sailor came through town, and he could play a lot of the Chet Atkins stuff. I watched him and said, 'Oh God, help me learn how to do that!' So I watched him real closely, learned it, and developed it." Though he flirted with the singer/songwriter mode of expression, Dykes felt the strongest resonance when playing unaccompanied guitar, and he quickly settled into his God-given niche as an instrumentalist. In his mid-teens, he added the banjo to his repertoire, and peppered his formidable guitar playing with banjospeak, engrafting frailing and rapid-fire chromatic single-note techniques. Traveling with his family, Dykes attracted increasing attention of gospel legend J.D. Sumner. Dykes was offered the opportunity to join The Stamps, Elvis' former backup band. Pulling up tent stakes, Dykes moved to Nashville and began touring with the group, but he soon became disillusioned. Disenchanted with some of the backstage antics, he returned home to Jacksonville, Florida, got a day job, and married Rita, his high school sweetheart.

Though Dykes settled into a nine-to-five routine, Providence was lurking around the corner. Setting off a chain reaction of ripe opportunities, 'Hee Haw' senior statesman Grandpa Jones performed at a festival near Dykes' hometown. Invited to audition, Dykes lost no time in trying out for Grandpa's band. This was Dykes' link to the Grand Ole Opry, where he later received his OJT in both traditional country and blues, in addition to sharing the stage with many of his long-time heroes, including Chet Atkins, Merle Travis, and Tennessee Ernie Ford.

Doyle can be seen in the two *Amazing Fingerstyle Techniques of Doyle Dykes* videos (MB96673VX and MB96674VX) and his solos are presented in the book *Dykesology* (MB98626BCD), all of which are distributed by Mel Bay Publications.

Gitarre 2000

Standard Tuning

Doyle Dykes

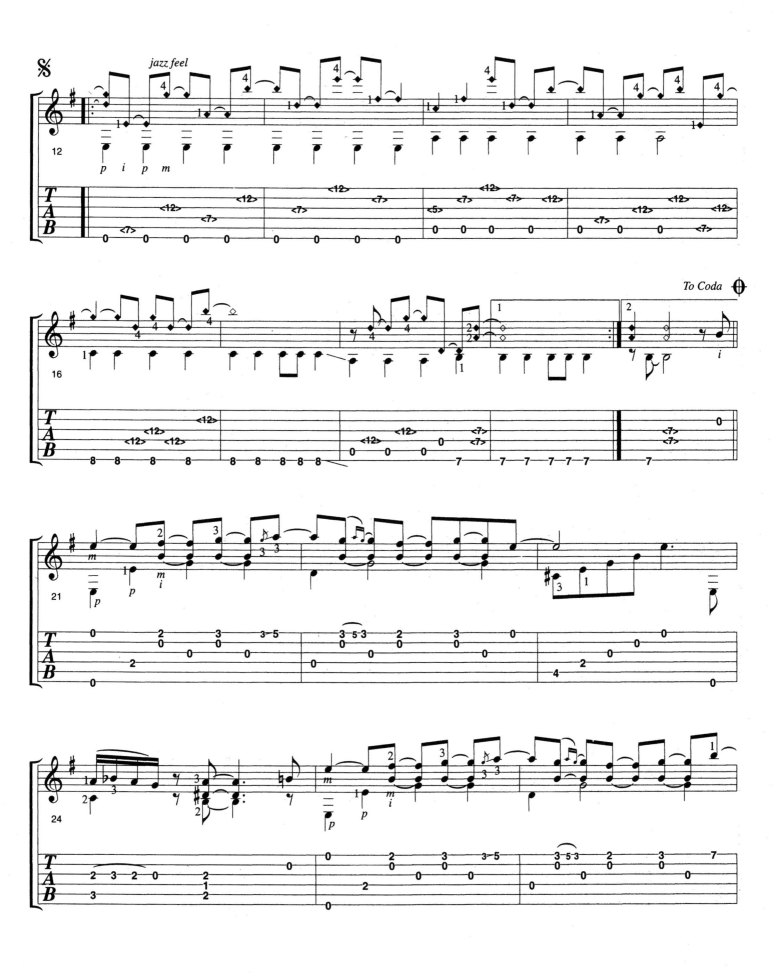

133

134

135

137

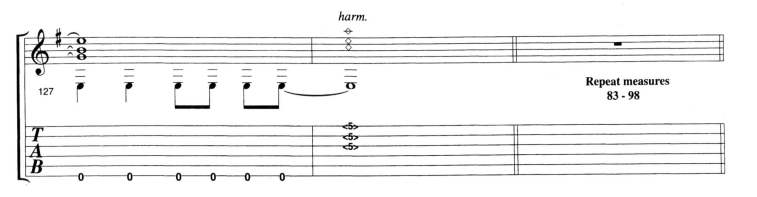

Repeat measures 83 - 98

Repeat measures 12 -20

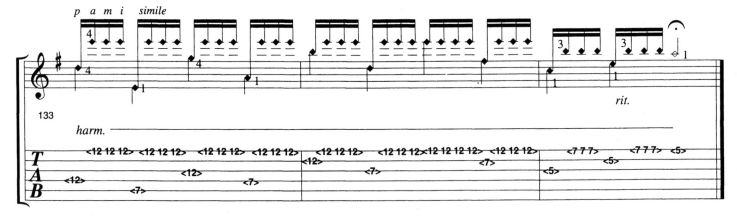

Steve Eckels

Steve Eckels has a Master's degree in guitar from the New England Conservatory and a Bachelor's degree in guitar from Berklee College of Music. He is a regular columnist for *Fingerstyle Guitar Magazine* and has written seven folios for Mel Bay Publications including, *American Love Songs and Ballads* (MB95265BCD), *Blues Classics* (MB95273BCD), *The Music of Stephen Foster* (MB95475BCD), *Gospel Classics* (MB95704BCD), *Music of the North American Indians* (MB96015BCD), *Cowboy Classics* (MB97250BCD) and *Gregorian Chants for Acoustic Guitar* (MB96651BCD).

Dove Song

Steven Zdenek Eckels

Used by Permission

144

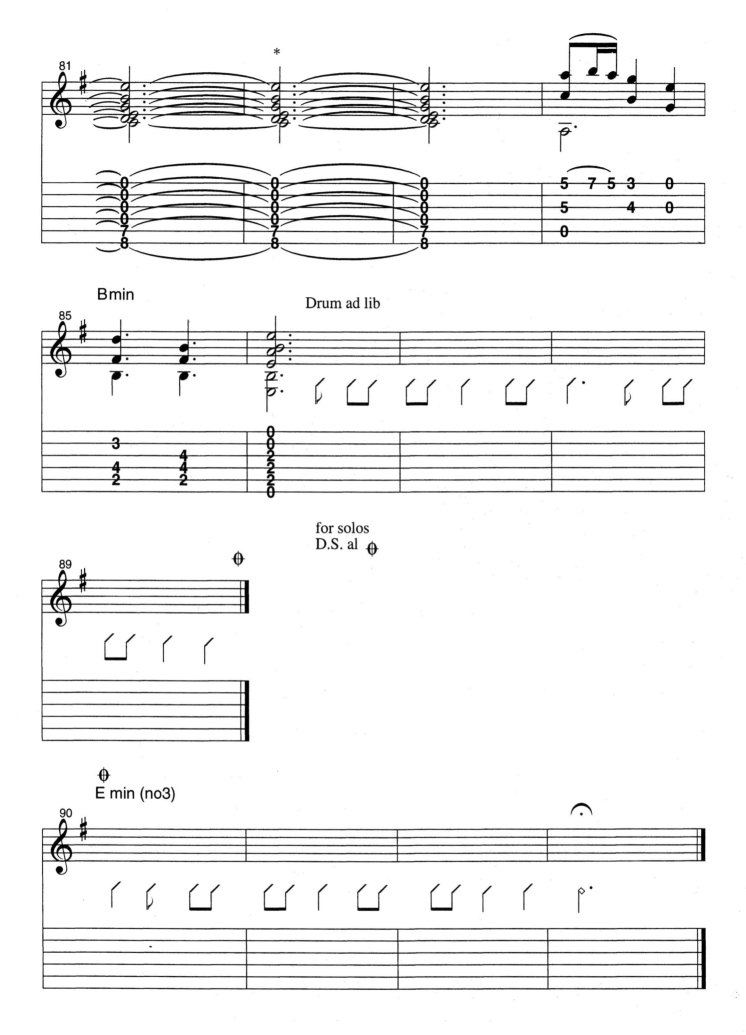

Tim Farrell

Guitarist, composer, vocalist, and performer Tim Farrell has touched and enriched the lives of many people. Tim performs con certs and does workshops around the country and has received extensive airplay on individual radio stations, as well as on nationally-syndicated programs including *Echoes, Acoustic Digest*, and *The World Cafe* in the U.S. and *Alphabet* in Europe.

Soon after its release, Tim's album *Skydancer* garnered airplay, accolades and sales around the globe. Billboard said "*Skydancer* resonates with soaring, memorable melody lines" and called Tim "a guitarist to be heard."

Tim's first solo album *Very* is such a beautiful example of intricate fingerstyle guitar playing that Tim was selected to be the first artist on *Guitar Fingerstyle - A Narada Collection*, a CD sampler of the finest fingerstyle guitarists working today.

Tim has been called "One of the new trailblazers - the bold ones who will take guitar into the next century." He is one of the select group of musicians who exemplify all that is excellent in their field and who have the unique ability to entertain their audience and inspire future generations of players.

A classical guitar major with a minor in piano, Tim understands well the intricate mechanics of music, yet his playing and original compositions display an elegant simplicity that celebrates the purity of the acoustic guitar.

A very active composer, Tim has written many solo and ensemble works for the guitar. He has provided the music for Multimedia Presentations, TV and radio shows, soundtracks, and interactive theatre productions.

Currently Tim is performing primarily as a solo artist in settings as varied as an intimate house concert to the 20,000 seat First Union Center in Philadelphia.

Tim is a member of the faculty of the Doyleston School of Music, teaches private lessons, offers workshops, and visits schools as part of his desire to further develop the knowledge, enjoyment, and appreciation of music. He believes that anyone can achieve fulfillment in music whether they are a casual listener, a serious music lover, a student, or a professional.

Joyride to Tranquility

Joyride to Tranquility is meant to be played with a joyous and relaxed energy. Let the open notes sustain as long as possible, letting the overtones overlap. On the second time through measures 19-34, pluck over the fretboard at approximately frets 16-20. On the second time through measures 95-102, pluck near the bridge.

Joyride to Tranquility

Double Drop D Tuning
DADGBD

Composed by
Tim Farrell

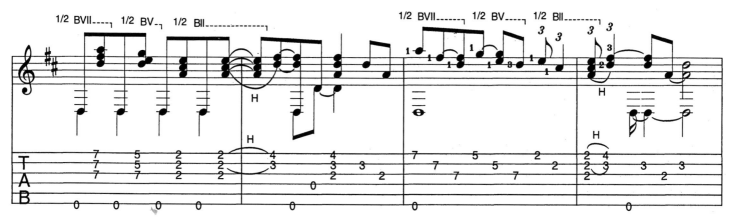

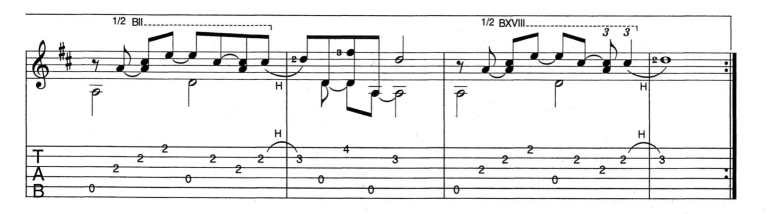

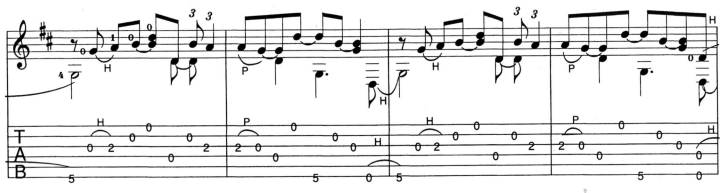

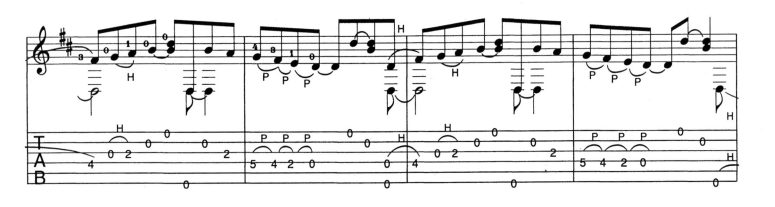

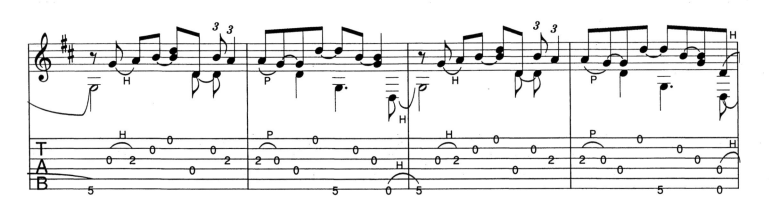

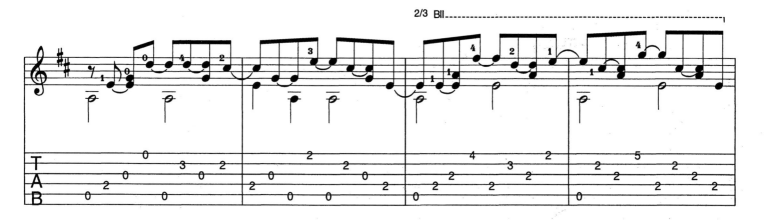

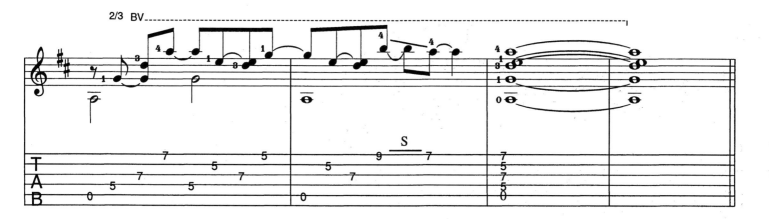

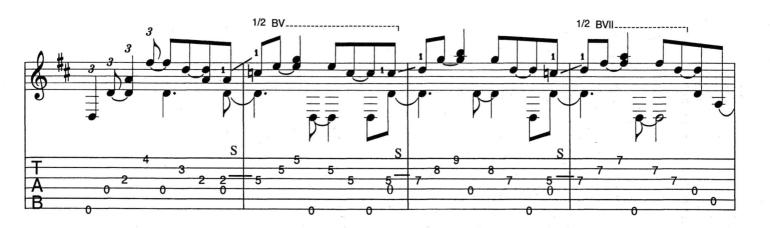

153

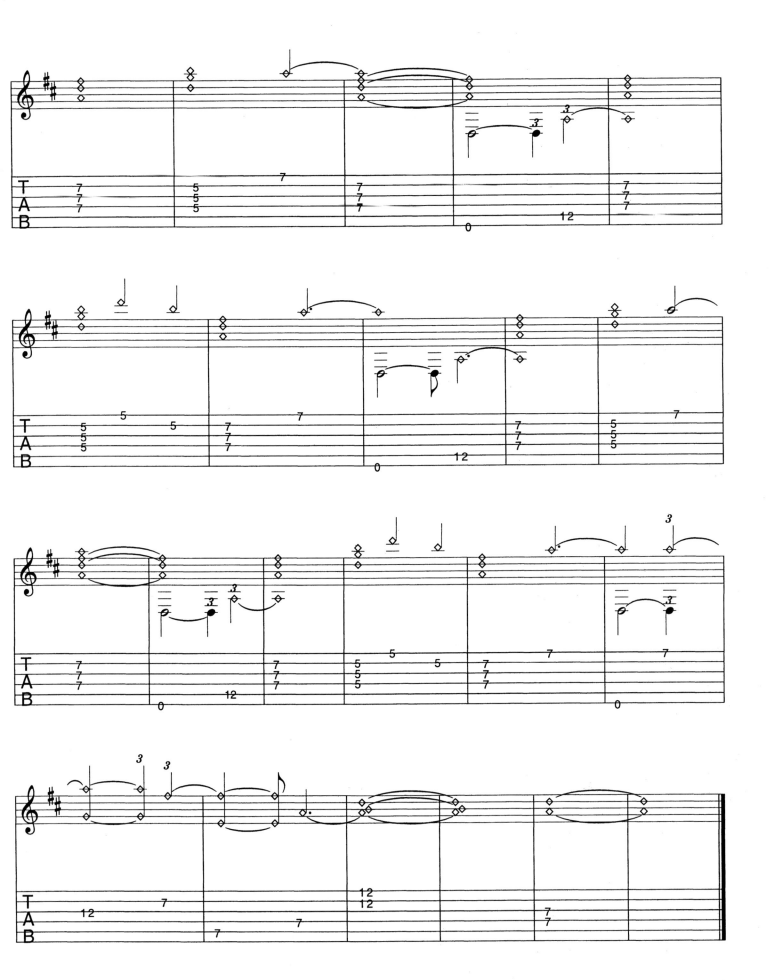

154

Peter Finger

Peter Finger has accomplished something few people achieve in our day: the perfect harmony of virtuosity, musicality and composition. His musical cosmos is boundless, showing profound knowledge of both music and the contemporary state of the art. The attentive listener will therefore encounter the language of *Debussy, Ravel* or *Stravinsky* time and again - and, in the same breath, perhaps find himself in the realm of rock. One can only marvel at Finger's almost orchestral, sometimes breathtaking, experimental tapestry of rhythm, harmony and melody. It should definitely be mentioned that all of these elements fuse together organically instead of just standing side by side without any connection. This is why Peter Finger's music is always a great sensual pleasure, far removed from any type of intellectual exercise - both demanding and stimulating at the same time.

Peter's solo collection, *The Guitar of Peter Finger* (MB96993BCD) is available from Mel Bay Publications.

Getaway

(From the album Between the Lines)

Peter Finger

guitar tuning: E - B - E - G - A - D

Capo: 2nd fret

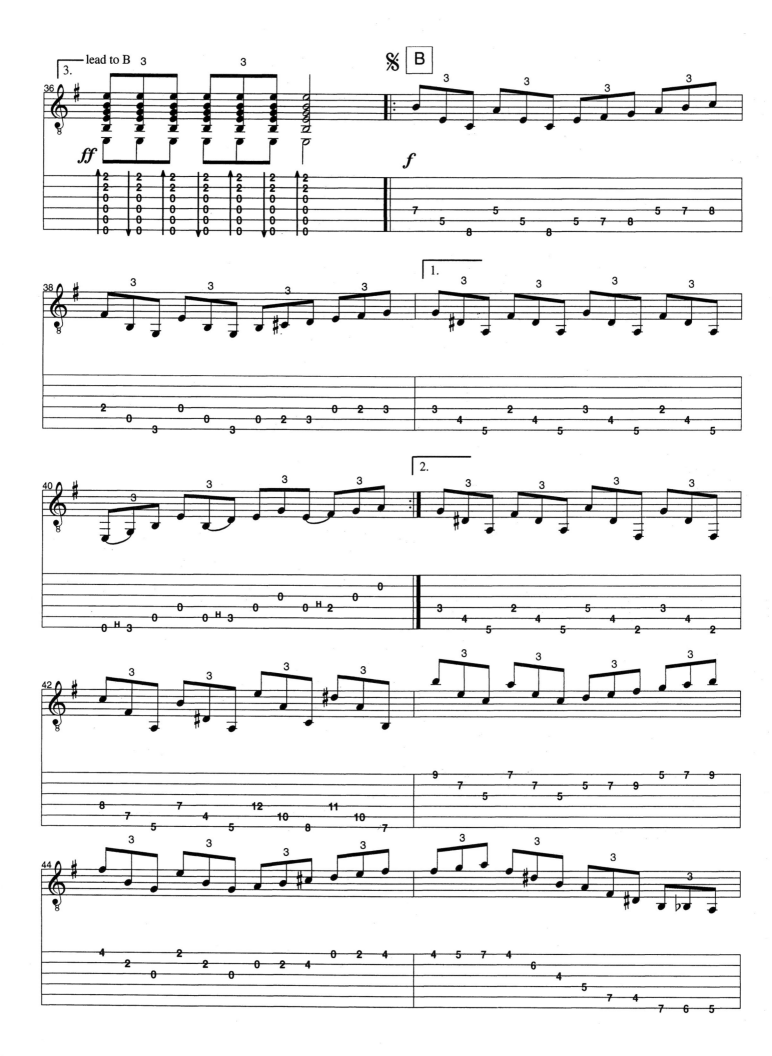

160

Tommy Flint

Tommy Flint is an outstanding guitarist who is known worldwide for his musical achievements. He is an internationally acclaimed author of guitar instructional books, CDs and videos. Tommy and his band have accompanied many major artists in concert halls, recording studios and package shows. He has shared the stage with artists such as Chet Atkins, Cher, Ray Charles, Roger Miller, Liza Minnelli, Dolly Parton and Glen Campbell. He and his band once performed as an opening act for the late Elvis Presley.

Tommy's resume includes performances at the Grand Ole Opry and Country Music Hall of Fame in Nashville, "A Tribute to Merle Travis" at the Ozark Folk Center in Mountain View, Arkansas, the Chet Atkins Appreciation Society (CAAS) in Nashville and the Walnut Valley Festival in Winfield, Kansas. He has performed at the Country Comfort festival in Ahtari, Finland and the World Guitar Expo in France.

Tommy has conducted clinics and workshops across the U.S. and Europe. He is well known for his work with the Music Educators National Conference, the Merle Travis Guitar Festival at Northeastern State University at Tahlequah, Oklahoma, the Home of the Legends Thumbstyle Contest, in Muhlenberg County, Kentucky, and the CAAS Convention in Nashville. He has participated in workshops with a number of internationally recognized guitarists including his cousin Merle Travis, Mel Bay, Thom Bresh, Bill Bay, John Knowles, Buster B. Jones and Muriel Anderson.

Tommy has written over 30 instructional books (with companion CDs) for Mel Bay Publications, Inc. Many of his books are used in the nation's leading music schools. Tommy's *Anthology of Fingerstyle Guitar* (MB93446), published in book form and recently released in the video format (MB94732VX), is the text of choice used for many years by the world's leading music teachers and guitar instructors. Two books in particular, one co-written with Chet Atkins and another with Merle Travis, are testimonials to both his writing and musical skills. He currently writes columns for *Fingerstyle Guitar* magazine and is often the subject of books and articles himself. He is featured in a chapter of *That Muhlenberg Sound*, a book that chronicles the musical history of this famous Kentucky county.

Tommy's honors include a Governor's Appreciation Certificate for his participation in Oklahoma Homecoming '90. He was commissioned a Kentucky Colonel by the Governor of the Bluegrass State and made an Honorary Police Chief by the Indiana Association of Chiefs of Police. He was proud to be designated a "Country Music Pioneer" by the Country Music Association and the Grand Ole Opry. A street in Drakesboro, Kentucky was recently named *Tommy Flint Avenue*. Tommy has, on several occasions, attended the Reunion of Country Music Artists by special invitation from the CMA. The highlight of one such reunion was when Tommy and legendary guitarist Mose Rager (Merle Travis' guitar mentor) took the stage to perform together. In 2002, Tommy was inducted into the National Thumbpickers Hall of Fame in Muhlenburg County, Kentucky.

As a youngster, Tommy absorbed much of the music from the coal mines and tobacco fields of Muhlenberg County, Kentucky, an area rich in the tradition of fine guitar music. Through the early influences of Merle Travis, Mose Rager, and "Spider" Rich, Tommy developed an unmistakable style of his own. In 1984 he returned to his Muhlenberg County roots to play at the prestigious Everly Brother's Homecoming festival and concert.

Tommy is heavily scheduled playing concerts with his accompanist, Margie Joines-Rhoads, conducting workshops and clinics, writing, recording and personally instructing a limited number of exceptional students. His performances, clinics, videos, books, CDs and tapes are an inspiration to guitarists and guitar music lovers the world over.

161

Aurora Borealis

Tommy Flint

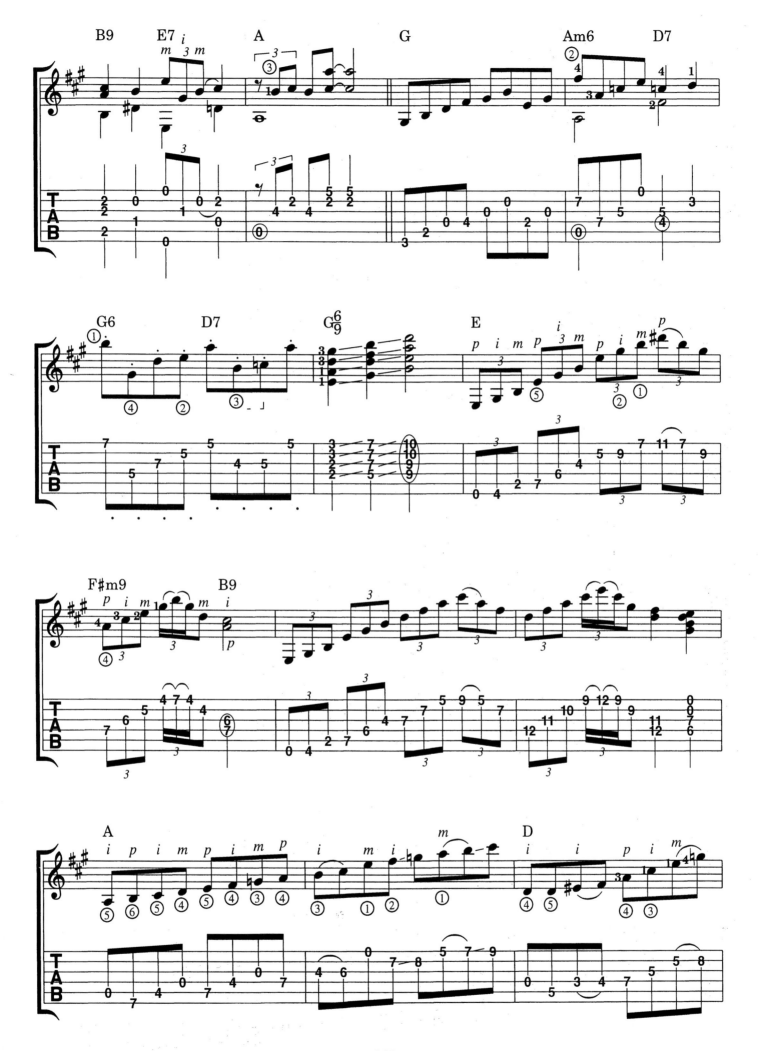

165

Rick Foster

Rick Foster is credited with being the first person to play a full concert of sacred music on the classical guitar. He was also the first to arrange and record an album of sacred music for classical guitar. That album, *Hymns for Classic Guitar*, was a milestone in guitar recordings, drawing rave reviews from critics and the public alike.

Rick was nominated by the Gospel Music Association for a Dove Award for Gospel Instrumentalist of the Year and has been a guest on the PTL Club and Three Angels Broadcast Network. Many of Rick's arrangements are published by Mel Bay Publications, and his columns appear regularly in *Fingerstyle Guitar Magazine*.

Rick resides in southern Oregon with his wife, Wendy, and their daughters, Jody and Tobi. When not on concert tour he spends much of his time arranging new music for the guitar. The Fosters are also avid organic gardeners, growing their own fruit and vegetables. Their garden was featured as a *Sunset Magazine* "Great Organic Garden."

Rick's solos can be found in the books *Favorite Hymns for Acoustic Guitar* (MB95438) and *Eternal Guitar* (MB95665BCD), published and distributed by Mel Bay.

Londonderry Air

(Traditional Irish Melody)

Arr. by Rick Foster

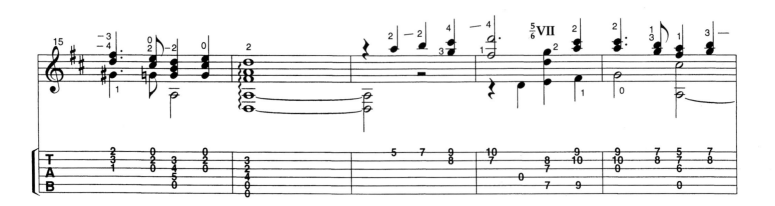

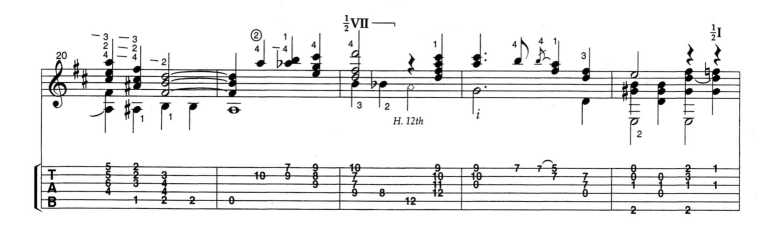

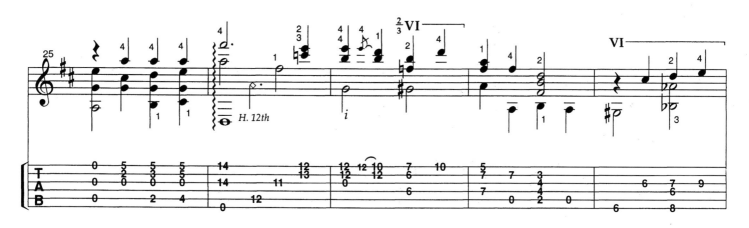

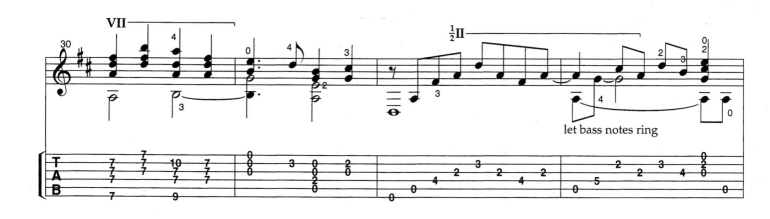

Some fingered eighth notes are not shaded
in as a reminder to hold as long as possible.

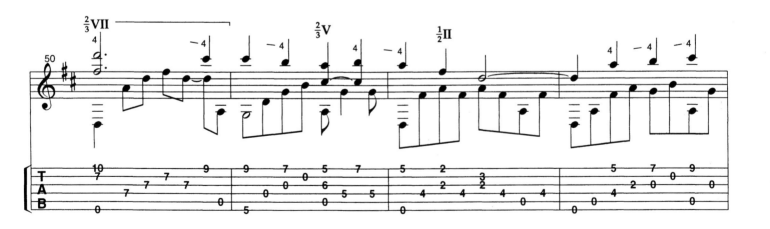

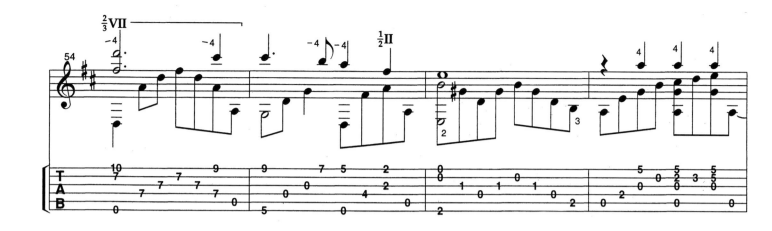

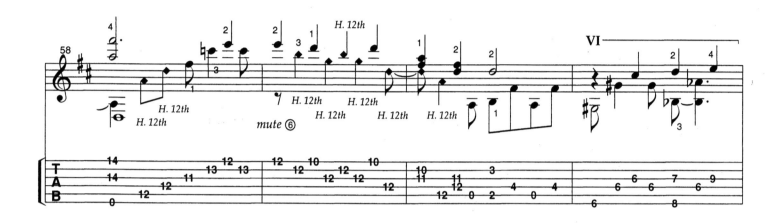

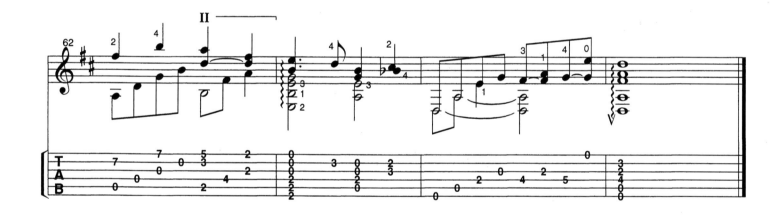

Stefan Grossman

Stefan Grossman has been recording, performing, and writing about acoustic fingerstyle techniques and styles for more than 30 years. During the period from 1965-1975 he studied and traveled with some of the legendary figures in the world of blues guitar. From this period came his landmark five-volume series for Oak Publications. Stefan has written many books and produced dozens of videos published or distributed by Mel Bay Publications. He recorded numerous solo albums for Shanachie Records.

Stefan's Mel Bay solo collections include *Legends of Country Blues Guitar* (MB95269BCD), *Complete Celtic Fingerstyle Book* (MB95217), and *Complete Country Blues Guitar Book* (MB94710BCD).

Blues for the Mann

By Stefan Grossman

CD #2 Track #7

STANDARD TUNING: EADGBE

INTRO

175

Ole Halén

Ole Anders Halén began studying electric guitar at age 13. By the time he was 15, he found himself in a touring rock band with several hit records. He was subsequently influenced by the playing style of Chet Atkins and at 17, in order to improve his fingerstyle technique, he began to study the classical guitar. On the recommendation of his teacher, Ivan Putilin, Halén studied classical music at the Sibelius Academy in Helsinki where he was later to occupy a guitar teaching position himself.

Captivated by the luthier's trade, Halén has constructed several classical guitars as well as being involved in guitar string production and music recording and publishing. He continues to show an intense love for all styles of music and has done much to popularize the guitar in Finland, serving as one of the organizers of the Scandinavian International Guitar Festival and as the organizer of the annual Midnight Sun Guitar Festival in Ikaalinen. With his involvement in so many facets of the guitar world, Ole Halén is one of Finland's most versatile guitarists.

Brusseler Spitzen

Albert Vossen
Arr. by Ole Halén

Used by Permission

Todd Hallawell

Todd Hallawell is a classically trained guitarist who, for several years, has been producing music for Soundset Recordings label where he is co-owner. He has recorded and produced internationally known solo artists as well as full orchestras. Encouraged by his clients, wife and friends to return to performing, Todd began entering competitions. In 1997, he won several in a row, most notably the Southwest Regional Fingerstyle Guitar Championship in Tucson, Arizona, and National Fingerpicking Guitar Championship at Winfield, Kansas. Since that time Todd's exceptional musical range has become well known throughout the guitar world. His album *Before My Time* has won critical acclaim.

Todd's expressive interpretations combined with his technical virtuosity provide a unique signature to his music, never more evident than in *Leola Kay*.

Continuing to compose and produce music, Todd lives in Scottsdale, Arizona with his wife Kay.

Leola Kay

Throughout this piece I use percussion to emphasize certain beats. I've chosen to include only the passages where the percussion seems more structural than ornamental.

In measure 13, the index (i) and middle (m) fingers of the right hand strum down lightly on the 2nd and 4th strings. Then a loud downstroke with the middle finger sets up the more percussive character of the B section.

In measures 16, 32, and 52, an F# can be played or muted with the left hand as indicated in the score.

In measures 22 and 26, a quick downstroke with the middle finger is used.

In measure 49 the 3rd beat is played as in measure 13. The second half of the 4th beat uses a downstroke with (m) followed by an upstroke with (i).

The symbol "T" is used to indicate the use of the thumb of the right hand in measures 42-45 and 58-62.

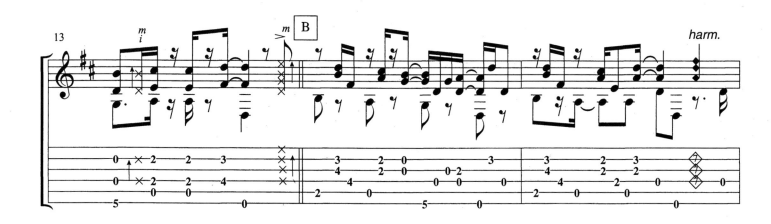
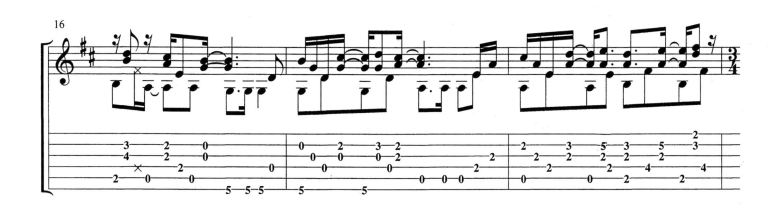

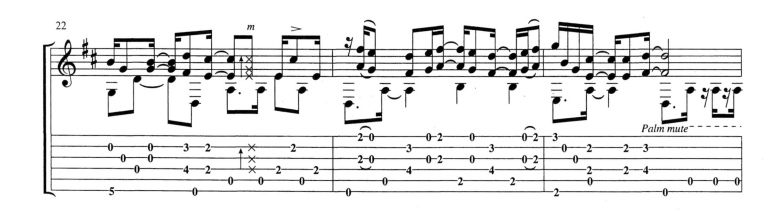

189

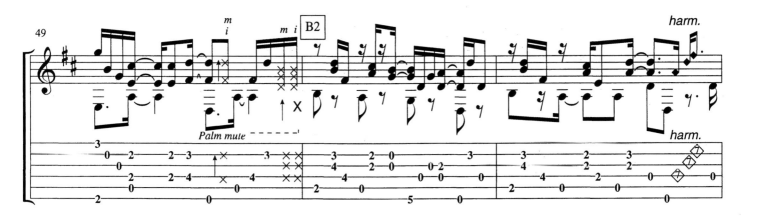

193

Roger Hudson

Born in 1961, Roger Hudson represents a new breed of classically-trained composer/guitarists. Hudson's approach is in the spirit of composers for the guitar such as Agustín Barrios-Mangoré, Fernando Sor, Mauro Giuliani, Francisco Tárrega and Leo Brouwer. All of these artists wrote as skilled composers but also as guitarists. So it is with Roger Hudson. Hudson draws inspiration from the past and the present to create unique music that is enjoyed by guitarists and the general audience alike. The Guitar Foundation of America's journal *Soundboard* spoke of "...many gorgeous moments..." and "strong themes" in describing Hudson's compositions.

Hudson began playing the guitar at age 12 in the Virginia suburbs of Washington, D.C. and learned the variety of musical styles that he draws upon in his works. He has studied guitar with John Sutherland, Christopher Berg, Fred Sabback, and in master classes with Christopher Parkening. Hudson studied composition with Charles Knox and Tayloe Harding at Georgia State University where he earned a Master's degree in music theory. He maintains a busy schedule of concerts, television and radio appearances, recording, composing, and teaching as well as being on the teaching staff at MARS Nashville. He currently resides in Nashville, Tennessee with his wife Brenda and two children, Camille and Elijah.

Roger's solo collection, *The Guitar Collection of Roger Hudson* (MB97747BCD), is available from Mel Bay Publications.

Blues from Jekyll

Roger Hudson

Swing ♩ = 138_158

D.S. al Coda

Jack Jezzro

Jack Jezzro is not a household name like a number of other Nashville cats, but a quick view of his resume tells you all you need to know about his background, his chops and the respect in which he is held on the studio scene there. He received a Bachelor of Music from Eastman School of Music, majoring in Double Bass Performance. He played double bass in the Charleston Symphony and Rochester Philharmonic Orchestras, before coming to Nashville in 1981 to play electric bass at the Opryland Live Shows and both instruments with the Nashville Symphony. He is an accomplished guitarist in a number of styles.

Beyond the Known

by Jack Jezzro

201

Buster B. Jones

Buster B. Jones' guitar has taken him to the far reaches of the world, not to mention all across the U.S. and Canada. The effect Buster has on an audience can best be described as a magical evening of music and back porch country humor.

What do the pro's say about Buster's self-taught picking?

"Buster is the best fingerpicker I've seen since Jerry Reed. He plays like he's double parked."- Chet Atkins (CGP).

"Buster B.'s talent is unmistakable. He's a monster player with chops galore, great ideas and an encyclopedia reservoir of guitaristic influences. One of the best players we've heard in years."- Guitar Player Magazine.

After an evening with Buster B. you'll see why they call him "the guitar player's guitarist."

Buster's solos can be found in the John August book, *Ballads & Barn Burners* (MB98627BCD) and in *Remembering Marcel* (MB99759) distributed by Mel Bay Publications.

Buster B. Boogie

Although this tune, in my opinion, is devoid of any musical value and can't be hummed or whistled, few pieces I play are as much fun!

It is laced with aggression, and is peppered with some unorthodox techniques, such as the use of all five fingers on the right hand (though the pinkie plays such a small part that it is hardly necessary).

This song is solely about the groove, so be prepared to tap your feet.

Buster B. Boogie

Buster B. Jones

Standard Tuning

208

209

210

211

Repeat Meas.
34 through 69

Repeat Meas.
70 through 71

Repeat Meas.
46 through 49

Repeat Meas.
105 through 112

Laurence Juber

Laurence Juber has been playing guitar for over 35 years. He was lead guitarist for Paul McCartney's *Wings*, winning a "Best Rock Instrumental" Grammy award for the track *Rockestra*.

At this writing, Laurence, known by guitar fans as "LJ," has released ten acoustic guitar CDs featuring his fingerstyle technique and extensive use of altered tunings. In March '99, he released a solo acoustic guitar album titled *Altered Reality* in the *Masters of Acoustic Guitar* series from Narada Records. His previous release, *Mosaic*, was recorded at Hollywood's legendary Capitol Studios. Mosaic showcases LJ's playing on acoustic and electric guitar in a variety of trio, duo and solo settings. Additionally a recording of the original composition *Liquid Amber* is featured on the windham Hill CD *Sounds Of Wood & Steel*.

LJ tours extensively in support of these releases with concert and clinic dates in the US and Europe. He is also featured, in collaboration with the unique guitar stylist Preston Reed, on the duo album *Groovemasters, Vol 1*.

He also enjoys continued success as a studio guitarist. He has worked on scores of television shows (*Home Improvement*, *Boy Meets World* and *Seventh Heaven*), films (including the academy award winning *Good Will Hunting*, *Pocahontas* and *Dirty Dancing*) and record albums (including collaberation with Ringo Star, Alan Parsons, Paul Williams, Al Stewart, Belinda Carlisle, The Monkees and Lou Rawls).

"One of the most gifted and versatile fingerstyle guitarists on the scene" –Acoustic Guitar

"Stunning fretwork"–Fingerstyle Guitar

"Poppy yet soulful, Laurence Juber is a master of timbral and dynamic shading. He draws you in like a seasoned storyteller."–Dirty Linen

The Jig Is Up

Tuning: DADGAD

Laurence Juber

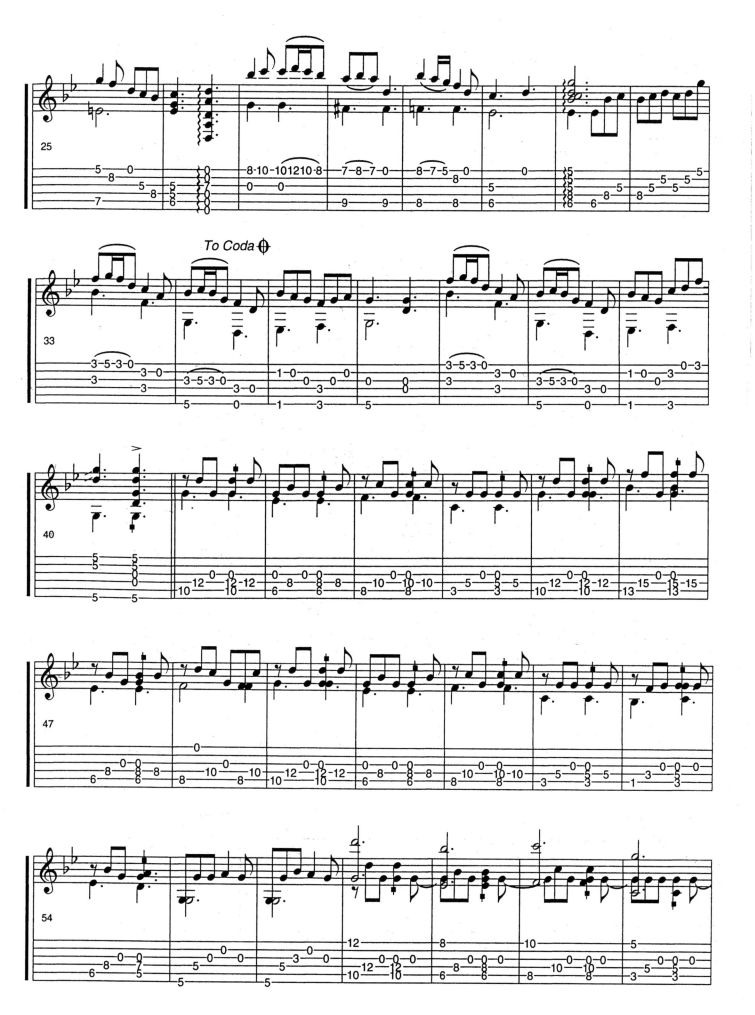

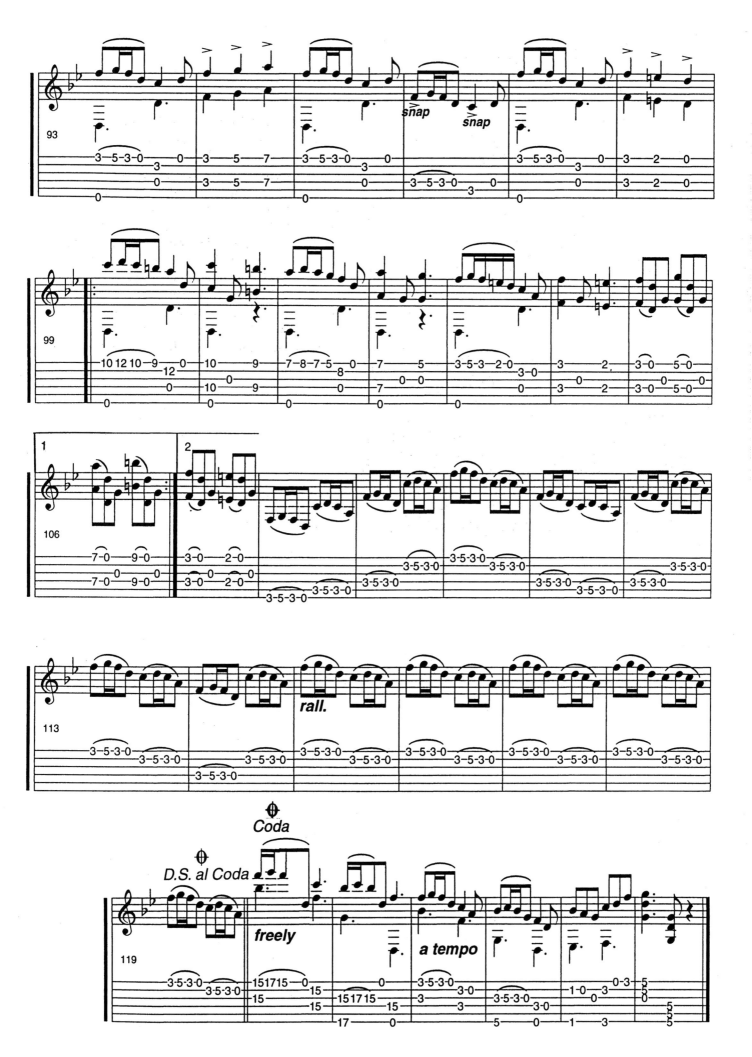

219

Phil Keaggy

Guitarist and songwriter Phil Keaggy has combined influences ranging from Haydn, Ravel, and Satie to Elvis, the Ventures, and Hendrix to forge a unique, personal style. Despite a lack of formal musical training, his exceptional talent has generated enormous critical and popular acclaim. Phil earned a Grammy nomination for his 1990 release *Find Me in These Fields*, and his 1988 album *Wind and the Wheat* won the "Instrumental Album of the Year" award from the Gospel Music Association. His 18 albums have helped earn him a place in *Musician Magazine's* listing of the "100 Greatest Guitarists of the 20th Century."

Segue/The Vision

Phil Keaggy

*Play freely. Phil used a volume pedal in conjunction with the tremelo arm
on his Parker Fly to create the Allan Holdsworthesque chordal swell effect.*

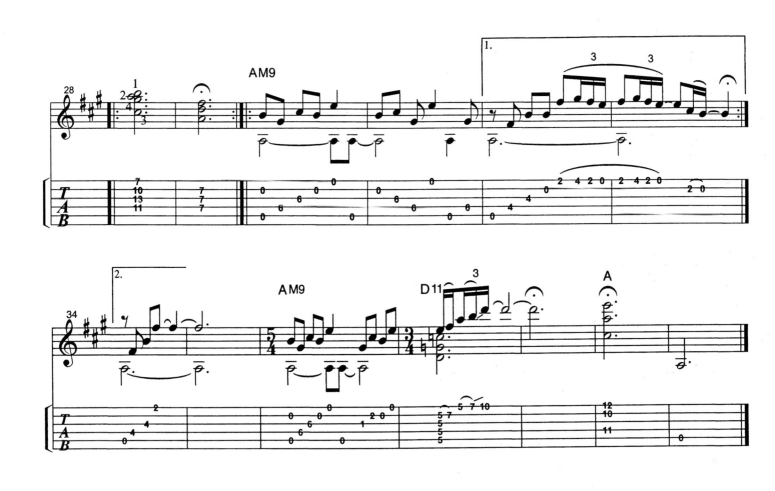

The Vision

DADGBE
Down 1/2 Step

Phil Keaggy

Repeat final measure
and fade.

Pat Kirtley

Pat Kirtley is a guitarist, composer, and recording artist, with releases on Narada, Rounder, and Mainstring Records. He is the 1995 National Fingerstyle Guitar Champion. Pat's compositions frequently have a traditional feel, but always incorporate cutting-edge guitar ideas and contemporary tonal structure. He was honored to be named one of "The Next Generation of Hot New Acoustic Acts" by *Acoustic Guitar Magazine* in the December 1997 issue, and John Schroeter, publisher of *Fingerstyle Guitar Magazine* characterized him as being "among the new trailblazers—the bold ones who will take the guitar into the next century."

Pat's new solo collection, *Kentucky Guitar* (MB97331) is published by Mel Bay.

Rural Life

This tune is built on three techniques, the banjo roll, Carter-style frailing, and cascading arpeggios. The first is the "banjo roll" as popularized on 5-string banjo by Earl Scruggs. The intro uses the banjo technique called a reverse roll. The right hand pattern is thumb - two - one, and the thumb alternates between the 3rd and 4th strings. This pattern is consistent throughout the intro.

The main melody (A) is played using a right-hand technique popularized by Maybelle Carter of the Carter Family. She would play the melody on the lower strings of the guitar using her thumb, and play rhythm along with it by brushing downward on the strings with her middle finger. It is a technique somewhat similar to the old-time "frailing" banjo style, but not quite the same. In my version of the technique, I am brushing downward lightly with the middle finger, and then coming back on the upstroke with a light brush from the index finger. It takes a lot of practice to get this right, and most of the challenge is in getting the stroke to be light enough. The index and middle fingers just barely touch the upper strings. Both the (A) and (A1) parts are played with this technique.

Part B uses the Scruggs roll technique again, this time on strings 5 through 2. The roll pattern for the right hand is exactly the same as in the intro.

Part A2 is the melody again, played up high on the neck, and with more of a Scruggs feel than parts in A and A1. It is important to play the notes very cleanly here, though there are a lot of them.

Part B1 is very similar to B, but watch for the differences. Part C uses a technique that some people call "cascading arpeggios". The right hand pattern for the arpeggio itself is index, thumb, middle. It is important to be consistent with the right hand pattern when learning this, because the notes are very quick, and you won't build up the necessary speed unless you use a consistent fingering on the right hand. Part D mimics the sound of a pedal steel guitar, and uses a chime harmonic at the 7th fret. It also employs the Scruggs reverse roll technique. Part A3 is a combination of A and A1. The tune then ends with a chime at the 7th fret.

Tuning
DADGAD

transcribed by
Bill Piburn

CD#2
Track#15

Rural Life

Pat Kirtley

228

229

230

231

Jean-Felix Lalanne

Jean-Felix Lalanne discovered the guitar at age twelve. Playing by ear, he spent many hours each day practicing. This, coupled with his innate musical ability, earned him his first solo concert only one year later. At fourteen he entered the Academy of Guitar in Marseilles, France where he studied classical guitar and orchestration.

In 1978 at 16 years of age, Jean-Felix won the prestigious French National Contest of Classical Guitar which presented him with credentials allowing him to study guitar anywhere in the world. The following year Jean-Felix moved to Paris where he began touring extensively, recorded his first solo album and became a much sought-after studio musician.

Acting as producer and arranger, Jean-Felix has recently completed the latest CD for French pop artist "Patsy" and is working on a new duet album with American guitarist Muriel Anderson.

Jean-Felix's duo arrangements as played with Marcel Dadi can be found in *Marcel Dadi & Jean-Felix Lalanne/Live at the Olympia 1988* (MB97521BCD) and on the book's corresponding video (97521VX). Jean-Felix also contributed a piece to *Remembering Marcel* (99759BCD).

Laguna Girls

The first part of this piece alternates a steady bluesy movement (measures 3 to 7) with more animated solos which become longer and more difficult. The X, measure 8, is a percussion on the 4th string. Try to make your guitar sound like a whole brass section, measures 15, 24, 29, to 41. The two-string pull-offs in measures 33 to 38 demand a lot of accuracy; don't let too many open-strings ring.

The second part is much faster. The difficult thing will be to keep that bass walking while playing the solo. Anything that looks like a barre above the 5th fret will be done with your little finger, left hand.

LAGUNA GIRLS

234

Laguna Girls

Jean-Félix LALANNE

242

Jay Leach

Jay Leach once worked as a salesman at the Guitar Center on Sunset Boulevard in Los Angeles. There he met studio wizard Jay Graydon. They became friends and Graydon began to recommend Jay for all kinds of performances. Jay made many other contacts during his time at the Guitar Center.

His life took a radical change when he considered going into the ministry. So for a year, his guitar stayed on its stand. Jay felt strongly called to be a musician, but on God's terms. Casual gigs continued to open up for Jay, and in '75 he began a two-year course of study with renowned chord chemist Ted Green. "I began playing solo guitar during the breaks," he says, "so I came to Ted with the tunes that I needed to learn, and he showed me chord substitutions galore. That whole experience was a fantastic on-the-job way to learn solo guitar. I never dreamed that years later it would come back to be such an integral part of what I do."

Needing to drastically hone his sight-reading skills, Jay began studying with a symphony conductor. It was at that time that his pedal steel skills proved helpful, and the doors of opportunity for studio work started to open wide. What really opened up the door was a gig as Barry Manilow's guitarist in '78. In '81, Jay became the guitar player in the John Davidson Show, during which he became fluent on five-string banjo, adding yet another instrument to his arsenal. The dam broke, and recording opportunities flooded in.

On Eagle's Wings

This very melodic piece incorporates both solo and accompaniment figures for the guitar. It has a smooth and easy listening quality to it that is quite appealing, but the easy sound is deceptive.

The pickup gives us a sense of the home key (G Major) but there is a bitonal quality to the first guitar passages. The G triad is played against a C in the bass, thus there is not a sense of resolve. This deceptive quality continues though measures 6-9, with the F Major 7 chord taking us farther away. This is an excellent example of a simple pattern becoming more complicated theoretically because of the use of different bass notes. Everything has a suspended quality. The cello, which maintains a pedal C at this point, serves to heighten this effect.

Also note that the left hand must move from a barre position at III to open position and back several times in the first section. Practice this move, and the accompanying right hand finger movements, slowly at first. Attempt the performance tempo only when you can play these passages cleanly and with confidence.

It is important to note that in musical terminology a "strong" progression of chords is not always desirable. C-F-G7-C, a la *Oh Susannah* or *This Land is Your Land* is an example of a strong progression. The style of On Eagles' Wings requires a softer, that is, less definite quality.

At measure 18, there is a change of function for the guitar, which now begins an accompaniment pattern that paves the way for the melody on cello. Measure 24 is where the G tonic first appears, and the contrast of a true tonic is very effective.

Other solo instruments include viola and guitar. There is much variety of timbre (different instrumental sounds and tone colors) in this piece. Thus there is not only some nifty picking we can learn but also something about how a successful arrangement is put together. Not a bad way to spend your practice session.

–Lenny Carlson

Form: Play measures 1-41, skip the measure indicated as solos, play measures 42-61. Take the repeat to measure 22. After measure 41 (2x) there is a solo section which is not included in the transcription for 40 measures. After the solos, play measures 42-61. Take the D.S. al Coda to measure 22. Take the Coda after measure 40.

On Eagle's Wings

By Jay Leach
Transcribed by Lenny Carlson

Capo at first fret

250

Paul Lolax

Paul Lolax is a Vermont-based musician and music instructor. He is a Stowe resident who has played guitar for more than 30 years. His career as a performer began in 1967 in Boston, Massachusetts, where he played solo and backup guitar at various coffeehouses and restaurants. *Broadside Magazine* voted him "Best Instrumentalist of the Year" in 1968. During the early '70s he toured the national college circuit, did studio work in Baltimore, Maryland, played in social service settings such as Boston's Charles Street Jail, and served as an artist-in-residence at independent schools in Massachusetts.

He has played with two groups and as a soloist in numerous home, church, wedding, restaurant, and social service settings since relocating to Vermont seven years ago. He also has appeared on the cable access program Vermont Folk Stage.

Paul was born in New York City and raised in Worchester, Massachusetts. He has written for *Acoustic Guitar* magazine, and wrote the book *Transcriptions of Scott Joplin and Joseph Lamb* (Hansen House). He recorded *Selected Works of Scott Joplin and Joseph Lamb* (Titanic Records). He studied classical guitar with Aaron Shearer at the Peabody Conservatory in Baltimore, and has played bass guitar and the mandolin in addition to acoustic guitar.

Paul's solos can be found in the Mel Bay book, *Guitar Solos in Open and Altered Tunings* (MB96326BCD).

Meadowlands

arranged by Paul Lolax

TUNING: DGDGBE

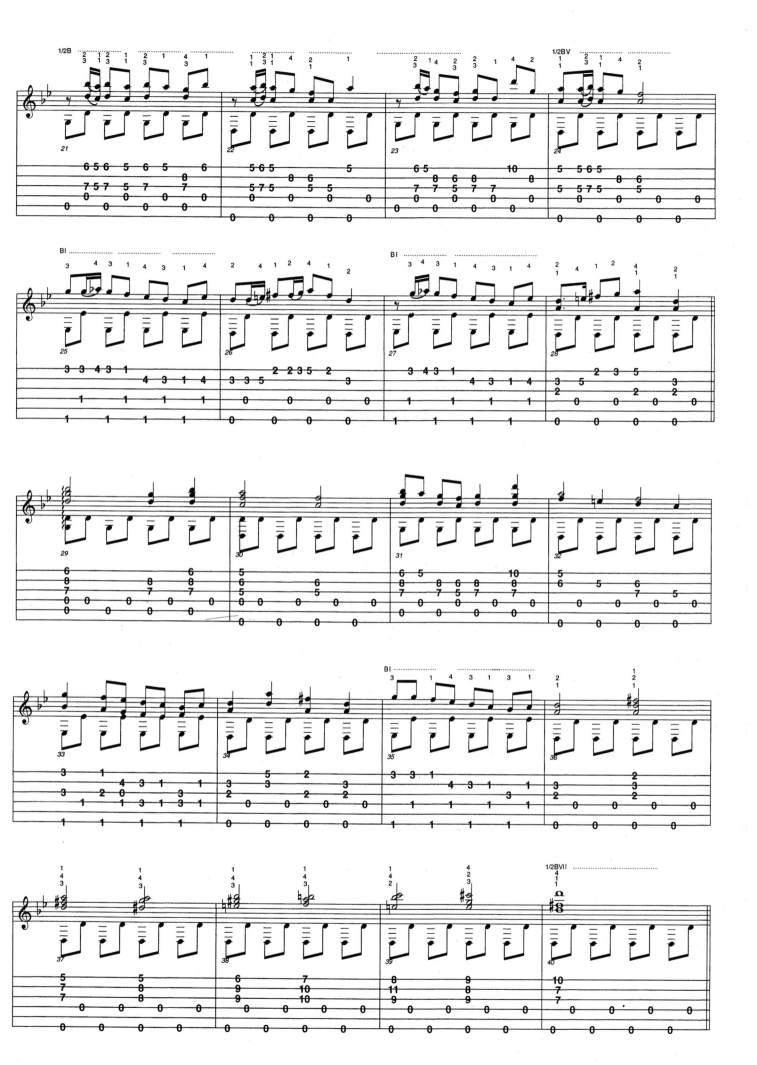

Woody Mann

Woody Mann has pursued a career as diverse as his abundant skills - ranging from playing with Jazz great Attila Zoller, serving as an accompanist for songwriter Dori Previn, to being a teacher to recording artist Paul Simon. He recorded regularly and performed everywhere from the orchestra pits of Broadway to festivals, concerts and club stages. Mann's reach as a teacher and writer has been just as sweeping; he has held master classes throughout Europe, been an instructor at the Augusta Heritage Center and Puget Sound Guitar workshop, a faculty member at the New School in New York City, and his writings about blues music and the guitar have appeared in many national music journals.

The remarkable ease with which Woody blends such a wide pallet of influences is evident on his two most recent recordings, *Heading Uptown* (featuring his talents as a vocalist, songwriter and guitarist) and *Stairwell Serenade* (spotlighting his solo guitar compositions) both of which have drawn international acclaim, as have Mann's extensive concert appearances throughout the United States and Europe. *Guitar Player* magazines review of *Stairwell Serenade* concluded with a simple one-word evaluation: "Phenomenal."

Mann has schooled countless guitarists through his popular books including, *Six Early Blues Guitarists, The Anthology of Blues Guitar, The Complete Robert Johnson* (MB95074BCD), and *Blues Fakebook*, and he has recorded a series of video tapes and CDs that focus on early master guitar stylists such as Lonnie Johnson, Big Bill Broonzy, Rev. Gary Davis, Blind Blake, and Eddie Lang. For Mann, their music is more than an echo of an earlier time: it is the creative standard that he continues to advance with his own improvisational music of today.

Top Hat

This charming and infectious piece is very Caribbean in flavor. The syncopation, phrasing and touch may remind the listener of Joseph Spence or possibly Blind Blake. The jaunty rhythms of the Piedmont and Island fingerpicking styles come alive in the inspired and capable hands of Woody Mann, well-known to students and aficionados of the genre as an outstanding performer and teacher.

The piece is in standard tuning with the 6th lowered to D. Some thumb damping occurs, on the 6th string especially. Such a timbre is percussive and serves to extend the range of the instrument in the ears of the listener. The first bass note is the pickup, on the & of 4. Notice how this sets everything off in a dancing rhythm. If the bass note had occurred on 1, (the downbeat), the whole feeling of the piece would be different, and a lot more square.

The bass notes are played very staccato for a kind of stop-time punctuation, and the rolling bass lines in the second melody section present a clever contrast. With the different touches in the bass and treble, the sense of true counterpoint is heightened, and the interplay of the voices is much more dramatic. All of the effects that Woody achieves are subtle, the result of many years of thoughtful practice and listening.

The C section (3rd melody) has the low D against a high f♯, an extremely open sound. All in all, Top Hat is a joy to practice, play and listen to. Hats off to Woody for his good humor and his imaginative use of the guitar.

–Lenny Carlson

Top Hat

Woody Mann

D.S. al ✪

D.S.S. to ✪ ✪

Interlude: ("Great Dreams from Heaven")

259

261

Dennis McCorkle

A few years ago, I was chosen as one of the top five hundred 'New Age' musicians in the world by Macmillian Press. Although I'm very pleased to be recognized for the music that I have written, I am more pleased to have had the opportunity to have music, and my modest gift for it, play such an important role in my life. It has always brought me great pleasure.

I'm also pleased that so many people have enjoyed the work that I've done throughout the years. Since the early sixties, when I left the piano and began playing and studying guitar, I have written more than fifty compositions and transcriptions for the instrument, numerous works for voice, orchestra, and concert band, and various instructional methods.

As a formally trained musician in both classical music and jazz, I have had some very fine teachers along the way including Frank Mullen, John Marlow and Dennis Sandole. Under their tutelage and influence I have developed a style that I believe combines both idioms. During the past thirty years, I have performed regularly as a solo guitarist and studio musician in the Washington, D.C., Atlantic City and New York areas.

The Green Valleys

265

*This page has been
left blank to avoid
awkward page turns*

El McMeen

El McMeen is an acclaimed fingerstyle steel string guitarist and teacher who took up the instrument as a freshman at Harvard in the mid-'60s. His artistry has been praised by numerous publications including the *Washington Post*, the *New York Daily News*, *Fingerstyle Guitar* magazine, and *Guitar Player* magazine. His playing is characterized by a sensitivity to melodic phrases and lyrical beauty punctuated by walking bass lines and innovative arpeggio and crosspicking techniques. El's music has been hailed by critics as "stirring....unbridled acoustic beauty" and "drop-dead gorgeous"- *Guitar Player* magazine.

El has also pioneered the use of the low-C tuning (CGDGAD) in the solo guitar repertoire. To date, he has written five Mel Bay solo guitar collections: *Acoustic Guitar Treasures* (MB97883), *Playing Favorites* (MB95973), *Solo Guitar Serenade* (MB95468), *Of Soul and Spirit,* and *Irish Guitar Encores* (94986VX) . He is also a co-author of *The Complete Celtic Fingerstyle Guitar Book* (MB95217) and has recorded three video guitar lessons for Stefan Grossman's *Guitar Workshop* series.

Jacob's Ladder

Arranged by
El McMeen

transcribed by
Bill Piburn

Tuning= CGDGAD
Capo II

CD #3
Track #2

*This page has been
left blank to avoid
awkward page turns*

Dale Miller

Dale Miller is a fingerstyle guitarist living in Berkeley, California with his wife and two cats. He spends his time writing feature and instructional articles for *Acoustic Guitar* magazine, teaching private guitar lessons, playing the occasional gig, serving as a computer consultant and trouble shooter for a San Francisco law firm and working at *Noe Valley Music*, the San Francisco guitar shop he co-owns. Mel Bay Publications has also released two other book/CD packages by Miller entitled *Dale Miller/Country Blues & Ragtime Guitar Styles* (MB96557BCD) and *Fingers Don't Fail Me Now* (MB96514BCD).

Whispering

CD #3
Track #3

Most intro chords written
for reference purposes only

adapted and arranged by
Dale Miller for solo guitar

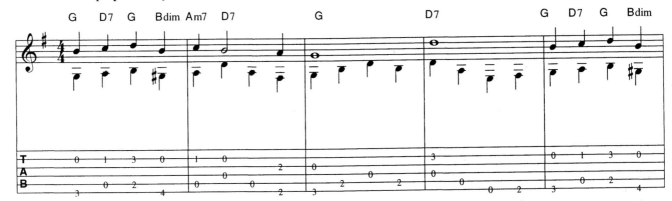

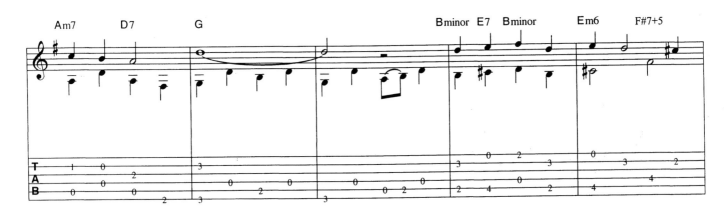

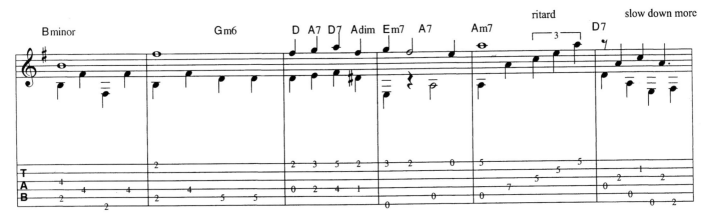

Used by Permission

273

Franco Morone

With a repertoire ranging from blues and Celtic tunes to jazz, Italian fingerstylist Franco Morone is recognized as one of the most gifted performers on the international guitar scene. Adhering to the concept of the "folk process" in which traditional music, while retaining its roots, evolves continually to remain fresh and current - Franco transforms diverse elements of folk music incorporating contemporary impressions. Through this process, his arrangements of traditional Irish and Italian folk melodies acquire a radically new and original quality.

Respected for the excellence and diversity of his work, Franco artfully blends echoes of the past with a variety of contemporary influences in his original compositions. His live performances can be quiet and reserved, or rousing and impetuous-but always mature and highly personalized. Franco regularly participates in international music festivals and frequently tours Europe, the U.S., and Japan in addition to maintaining a rigorous teaching schedule of private students, workshops, and magazine columns.

Crazy Basses

Swing
(Triple feel to beat)

275

To Coda

276

D.C. al **Coda**

Coda ϴ

279

Stevan Pasero

Critically acclaimed as a "pioneer for the guitar repertoire," Stevan Pasero is fluent in a variety of guitar styles including classical, flamenco, New Age, jazz, Latin, and Brazilian. Born in 1954 in San Francisco, he began playing guitar at the age of 10, initially focusing on classical technique but later diversifying into jazz and flamenco. Pasero studied with various teachers and concert artists and attended San Francisco State where classes in musical analysis, harmony, and composition led to post-graduate work in transcription. "Transcription is a tedious, meticulous task," he explains. "You have to melt down 40-80 instruments into four or five notes. I utilize this technique in my compositions resulting in a synthesis of styles within my original works."

Mr. Pasero is featured on seventeen recordings and has produced approximately forty studio recordings by other artists. He has written well over 500 compositions and transcribed more than thirty major symphonic works including *The Nutcracker Suite* for guitar, also published by Mel Bay Publications.

Gitana

by Stevan Pasero

*This page has been
left blank to avoid
awkward page turns*

Ken Perlman

Ken Perlman is considered one of the top clawhammer banjo players in the world - known in particular for helping to develop melodic clawhammer, which has transformed clawhammer from an accompaniment to a solo style of banjo playing. As can be heard on his recordings *Island Boy, Devil in the Kitchen, Live in the U.K.*, and *Clawhammer Banjo & Fingerstyle Guitar Solos*, his lively, authentic adaptations of reels, jigs, hornpipes, strathspeys and other Celtic tunes are especially worthy of note.

Ken has produced some of the most widely respected banjo instructional material of modern times. Some of these include the book and video set *Clawhammer Style Banjo* (Centerstream), the books *Melodic Clawhammer Banjo* (Music Sales) and *Basic Clawhammer Banjo* (MB95548BCD), and the videos *Beginning and Intermediate Clawhammer Banjo* (MB95592VX; MB95593VX). He has also been writing a clawhammer column for Banjo Newsletter for over 15 years.

An active folklorist, Ken spent over a decade collecting tunes and oral histories from traditional fiddle players on Prince Edward Island in eastern Canada. In 1997 he received an award in publishing from the Prince Edward Island Heritage Foundation for his tune-book *The Fiddle Music of Prince Edward Island* (MB95393).

Sonny's Mazurka

Named for Sonny Brogan, a well-known button accordion player of this century, this tune has very strong accents on the first beat of each measure and should be played spiritedly. On [The Chieftains, No. 3] (Claddagh Records No. TA5). Medium tempo with attention to phrasing.

Sonny's Mazurka

Key of D major (tune 6th to D)
3/4 time

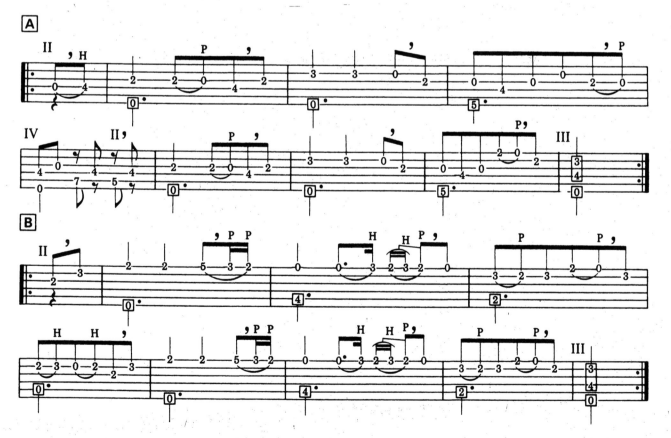

Al Petteway

A master of "fingerstyle" playing, Al Petteway fuses Celtic ideas and tunings with American themes and drive. His captivating melodic compositions appeal to music lovers of all ages and his warm stage presence combined with a charming sense of humor delight capacity audiences at every performance. The Washington Area Music Association has awarded him with no less than 18 "WAMMIES" including the top prizes of Musician of the Year, Artist of the Year and Best Instrumentalist.

His reputation as a first-class accompanist has been earned through work done on stage and in the studio with artists such as Grazz Matazz, Peter Rowan, Debi Smith, The Smith Sisters, The New St. George, Maggie Sansone, Bonnie Rideout, Susan Graham White, Grace Griffith, Cheryl Wheeler, Tom Paxton, and Jonathan Edwards. Released internationally on the Maggie's Music label, his solo recordings, *Whispering Stones*, *The Waters and the Wild* and *Midsummer Moon* have now firmly established him as one of the world's premier acoustic guitarists.

Al's books published by Mel Bay include *Caledon Wood* (MB96930), *Whispering Stones* (MB95381), *Midsummer Moon* (MB95552), *The Waters and the Wild* (MB95608), and *A Scottish Christmas for Guitar* (MB96783).

A Waltz for Rebecca

DADGAD, Capo 5

Al Petteway

From Maggie's Music *Caledon Wood* (MM217) www.maggiesmusic.com

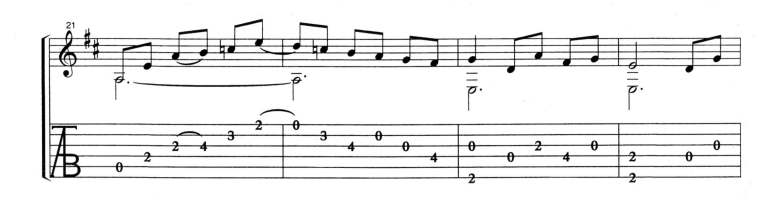
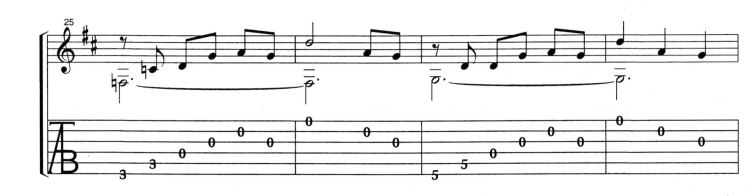

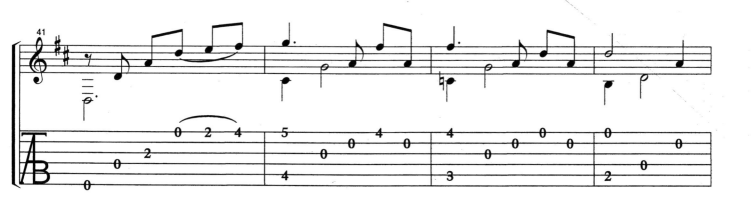

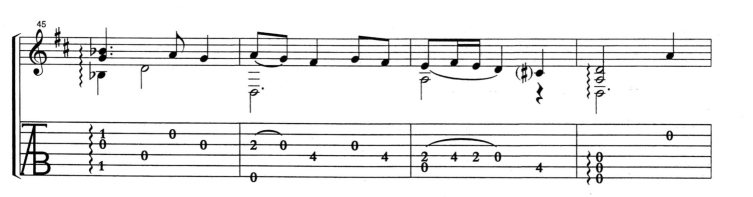

slightly slower

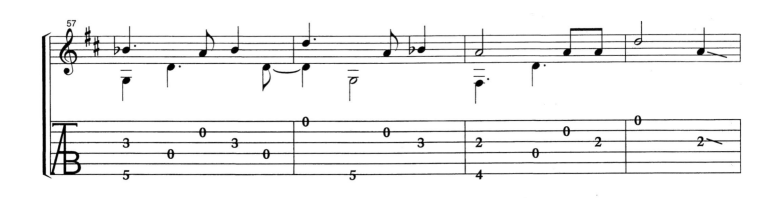

D.C.
2nd time D.S. al Fine

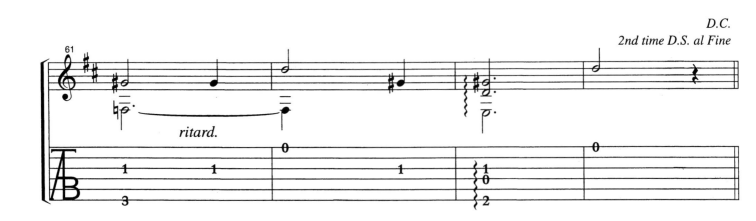

Bill Piburn

A native of Kansas City, Missouri, Bill Piburn now resides in Nashville, Tennessee where he leads a creative life as a guitarist, author, transcriber/arranger, music typesetter, and editor of *Fingerstyle Guitar* magazine. Bill studied classical guitar with Douglas Niedt and Christopher Parkening and in a master class with Pepe Romero. Bill undertook additional jazz studies with pianist John Elliott. Bill's transcriptions have appeared in numerous Mel Bay Publications books as well as in *Acoustic Guitar* and *Just Jazz Guitar* magazines. He is the author of Mel Bay's *Complete Book of Fiddle Tunes for Acoustic Guitar* (MB95471), *French Music for Guitar* (97064BCD), and *Fingerstyle Guitar Gig Book* (96196).

Bill's performance and arranging skills have won praise from such celebrated guitarists as Martin Taylor, Charlie Byrd, Jorge Morel, Chet Atkins and Jack Wilkins. He made his recording debut with the *American Heritage Society* in 2000 with a collection of Christmas tunes called *Cuna de Navidad (Christmas Cradlesong)*.

[Bill Piburn is] one of the best arrangers, players, and teachers I have known.

-Chet Atkins

Jesus Loves Me

Arranged by
Bill Piburn

294

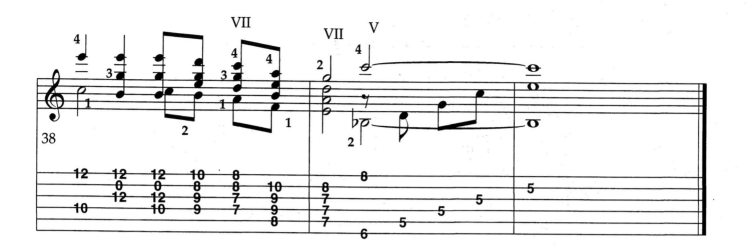

Chris Proctor

Call the guitar playing clean, bright, and emotive. Describe his compositions as innovative, elegant, and rich in texture. Trace the roots of his style to folk, jazz, and even classical music, and, when all else fails, categorize his playing as Baroque folk. Go on and compare him to Leo Kottke and Michael Hedges, but even then you will not have completely captured Chris Proctor and his fingerstyle guitar playing.

In his taut, faceted compositions, Chris gives the guitar sole responsibility for a piece's rhythmic, melodic, and harmonic components, and in the process creates full-voiced "guitar songs." His playing illuminates the instrument's deepest voices and most sonorous qualities, rendering a pop-folk equivalent of the classical guitar sonata.

Most original music, if it really lives up to the word, is hard to classify. It is often composed of unique ingredients, stirred by the writer's creative imagination, and must defy easy pigeonholing. With that disclaimer, here is what can be said of Chris Proctor:

• He is an acclaimed composer of original music whose chosen voice is the steel-string guitar.

• He is an innovative guitarist and recording artist of the highest order, and an extraordinary performer with a gift for communicating the tremendous variety, vitality, and accessibility of his compositions.

• He coaxes sounds from his instrument that belie the guitar's "everyman" reputation.

• His compositions span an entire spectrum of folk, jazz, classical, and ethnic sensibilities.

Besides his seven CDs on *Flying Fish* and *Windham Hill*, his recent books, videos, and endorsements testify to Chris's standing as one of the elite fingerstyle composers and performers of the day.

Chris's live and recorded work has attracted high praise from listeners as well as critics and reviewers, who have found it challenging to describe and neatly label his music. All you really have to do, however, is listen and enjoy.

Runoff

Runoff is a difficult song, and the crux of it is the four bar phrase which starts out slowly in the introductory section and is echoed at full speed immediately thereafter, eight bars into the C section. Expect to spend a little time with those bars, and with both the right and left hand parts of the puzzle. In fact I'd be chagrined if you didn't, because I certainly had to. If those bars fall into place, the rest will come along. Try and make the piece sound joyful.

This song is also written in my current favorite tuning, DADGBD. Perhaps my earlier comments about its advantages are making a little more sense now. The phrase mentioned above would have been next to impossible to play without a tuning like this.

Runoff

Capo at 2nd fret

Chris Proctor

Tuning: DADGBD ♩ = 120

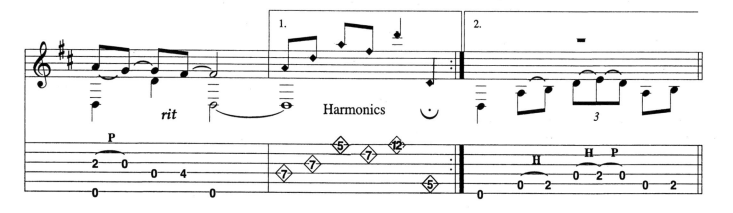

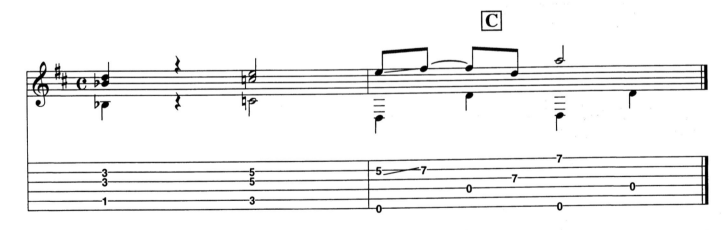

REPEAT LAST FOUR BARS TWICE.
SECOND TIME QUICKLY

303

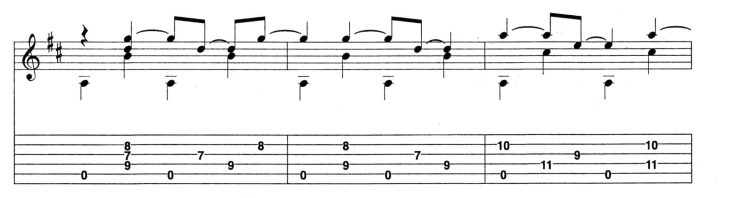

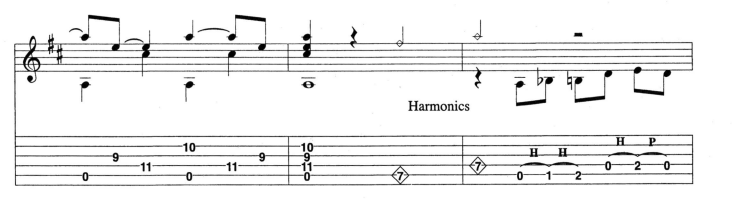

Harmonics

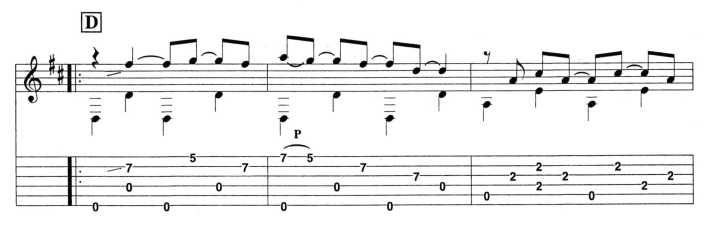

D

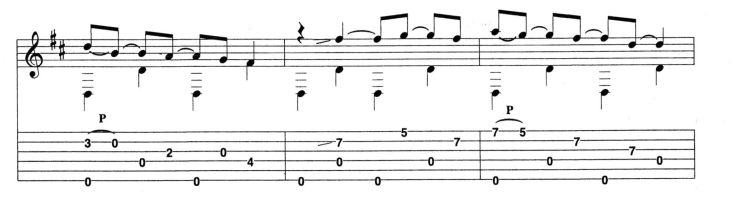

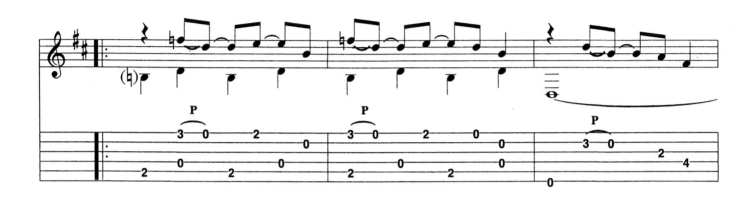

Variation on D

307

RETURN TO AND REPEAT D
THEN GO TO ENDING

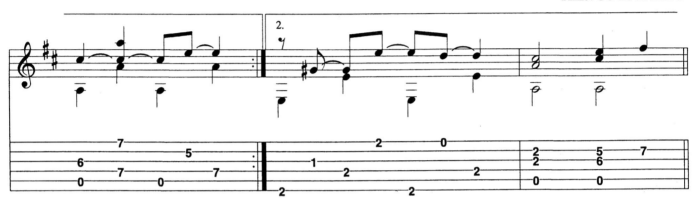

Ending

REPEAT LAST TWO
BARS TWICE.

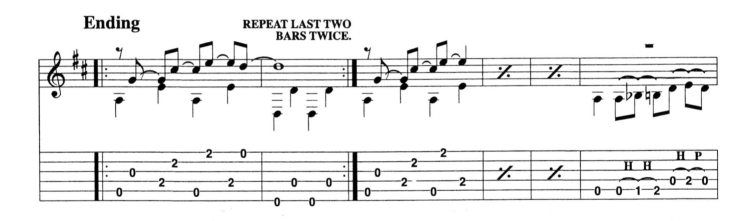

Harvey Reid

Songwriter and multi-instrumentalist Harvey Reid has honed his craft over the last 30 years in countless clubs, festivals, street corners, cafes, schools, coffeehouses and concert halls across the nation. One critic called him "the renaissance man of folk music." He has absorbed a vast repertoire of American music and woven it into his own colorful, personal and distinctive style. His 13 solo albums on Woodpecker records showcase his mastery of many instruments and styles of acoustic music, from hip-folk to country, slashing slide guitar blues to bluegrass, old-time, celtic, ragtime and even classical.

Reid's skills and versatility with the guitar alone mark him as an important new voice in acoustic music. He won the 1981 National Fingerpicking Guitar Competition and the 1982 International Autoharp Contest. Yet he's also a solid flatpicker who has won the Beanblossom bluegrass guitar contest, a versatile and engaging singer, a powerful lyricist, prolific composer, arranger and songwriter, a solid mandolin and bouzouki player, and a seasoned performer and entertainer. He recorded the first album ever of 6 & 12-string banjo music. His 1990 album *Steel Drivin' Man*, was chosen by *Acoustic Guitar Magazine* in 1996 as one of 10 Essential Folk CDs of all time, along with recordings by Woody Guthrie, Joan Baez and other hallowed names. His music was included in the blockbuster BBC TV show Musical Tour of Scotland, and he was featured in the *Rhino Records Acoustic Music of the '90s* collection, along with a "who's who" line-up of other artist including Richard Thompson, Jerry Garcia & Leo Kottke.

Although Reid has been somewhat reclusive, his reputation as a musician's musician is spreading fast. He has become a featured act at many of America's premier concert clubs and festivals, including the Telluride Bluegrass Festival and the Walnut Valley Festival. Radio DJs and critics nationwide are discovering his remarkable recordings, (which have sold nearly 100,000 copies!) and audiences coast-to-coast are flocking to catch his exciting performances.

You'll find elements of the traditional troubadour, the modern poet-songwriter, the American back-porch picker, the classical virtuoso, and a bit of Will Rogers style dry humor and satire. You'll hear folk, country, classical, blues, ragtime, rockabilly, celtic, bluegrass, and popular music influences. Reid has a vast repertoire of traditional and contemporary songs, and weaves them seamlessly together with his own compositions and wry humor.

Don't miss a chance to hear the Master Minstrel in concert!

Prelude to Minstrel's Dream

This is the first section of a 23-minute guitar piece I first wrote in April 1984 and recorded in October of 1986. The Prelude *is an exploration of the use of the Esus configuration of a partial capo that illustrates how the counterpoint bass and treble lines, which strongly suggest a Baroque style, play against the ringing drone strings set up by the partial capo. If you tried to do this with an open tuning, you would not have the scale facility to play the various runs, and without the partial capo, the guitar would not sound so resonant. It requires a pretty good left hand to play, but is no harder than some of the basic Bach pieces that beginning classical guitar students learn. I think it is more "guitaristic," and it is very satisfying to play.*

Prelude to Minstrel's Dream

Form = AABBCCBA

by Harvey Reid

©1984 by Harvey Reid (Quahog Music BMI)

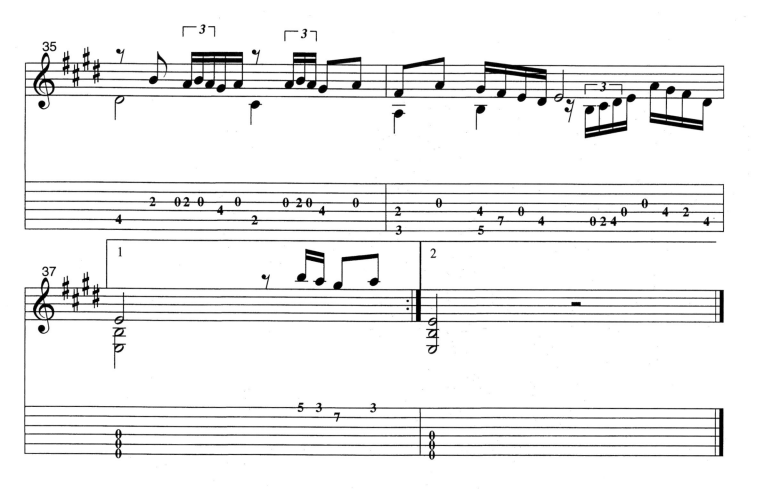

John Renbourn

Born in 1944, Marelebone, London. Studied music at George Abbott School Guildford and classical guitar at the Guildhall. Attended Kingston Art School in the early sixties along with Eric Clapton and Sandy Denny.

Recorded with American singer Dorris Henderson in 1964, followed by first solo album *John Renbourn* for the Transatlantic company. Collaborated with fellow Transatlantic artist Bert Jansch on *Bert and John* a collection of duets that acquired the label "folk-baroque." Formed *The Pentangle* with Jansch, touring and recording between 1967 and 1973 including appearances at The Filmores, Newport Folk Festival and Carnegie Hall.

Guitar based solo projects included *Sir Jonalot of Merrie England, Lady and the Unicorn, The Hermit, Black Balloon* and *Nine Maidens*. From the mid-seventies toured and recorded with Stefan Grossman and formed the "John Renbourn Group" recording British folk based material, *A Maid in Bedlam* and *Enchanted Garden*. Enrolled at Dartington College in 1979 to study orchestration and composition. Took up a post at Dartington heading a course in guitar studies. Continued as a solo performer, including a shared concert with Doc Watson at Carnegie Hall, while devoting more time to composition.

More recent projects have been the group "Ship of Fools" formed for a Central Park Summer Concert and collaborations with Archie Fisher and Robin Williamson, which produced *Wheel of Fortune*. Publications include *Original Guitar Solos, Guitar Styles* (Oxford University Press), *Anthology of O'Carolan Music* (MB95266BCD) and *Complete Anthology of Medieval and Renaissance Music for Guitar* (MB95394). Both the "John Renbourn Group" and the "Renbourn Williamson" duo received Grammy Award nominations. Shanachie records released the latest solo project *Travelers Prayer* last year.

Palermo Snow

Form = Intro AAB(1st)CB(2nd)DAB(last time)

John Renbourn

Tuning - D A D G B♭ E

Fast and Flowing

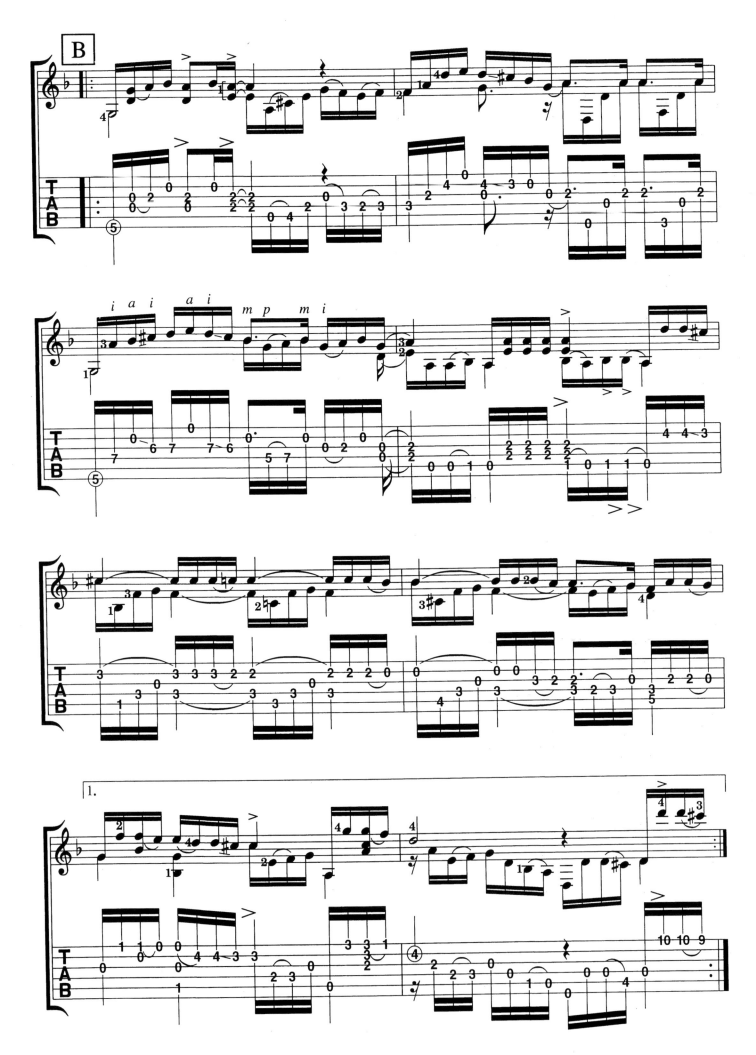

316

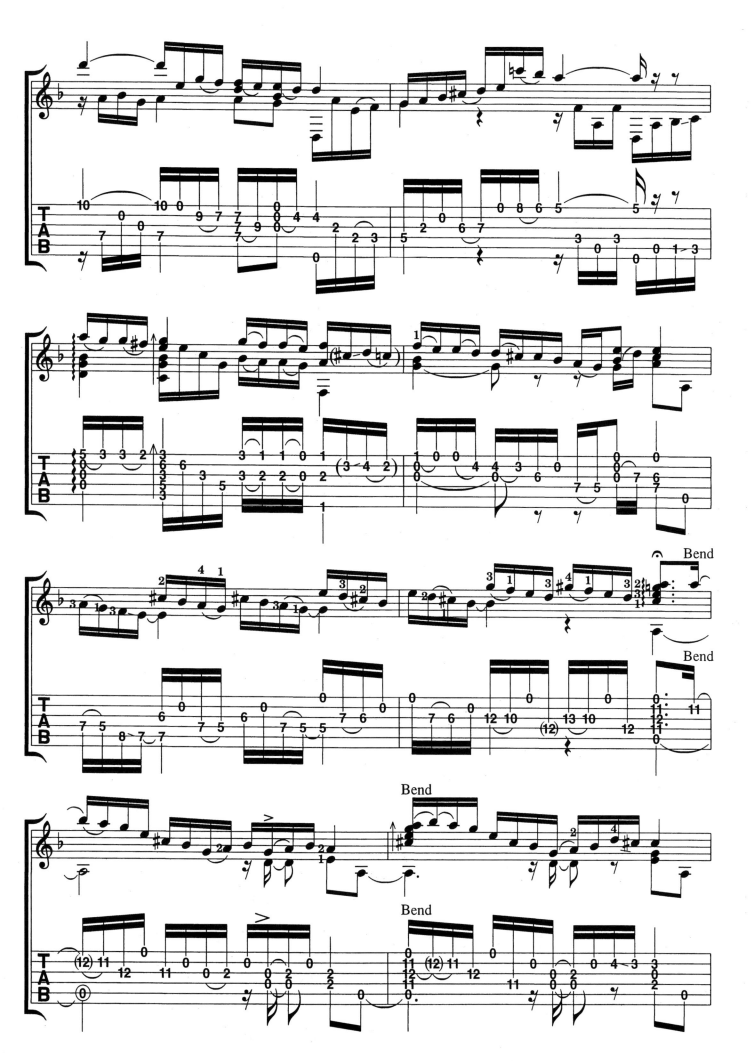

Da Capo to Last time

320

Don Ross

Since the dawn of classical guitar in the late-eighteenth century, players have struggled to defy physics and make six strings sound like a small orchestra. In the days of Fernando Sor and Mario Giuliani, the only way to accomplish this sleight of hand was with masterful finger-style technique. Though our tools have changed over the last 200 years, the task remains just as daunting. Fortunately, three recent releases confirm that the "fretboard orchestra" is alive and well.

Canadian Don Ross is a two-time winner of the prestigious National Fingerpicking Championship held annually in Winfield, Kansas. Listening to *Passion Session* (Narada), a captivating collection of acoustic solos, it's easy to hear why he's a champ. In every piece, Ross puts his stunning technique in service of the composition. For many talented pickers, the tune is an excuse to display dazzling technique. Not so with Ross. There's a lot going on–rippling harmonics, funky tritone riffs, jazzy chord substitutions, walking bass lines, percussive knuckle whacks, and liquid runs composed of alternating fretted and open strings–but he plays with such a relaxed groove that it's easy to surrender to the music.

In addition to extracting sweet timbres from a jumbo Lowden, Ross dips into the lower registers to draw twangy tones from a custom Oskar Graf 7-string and a custom Marc Beneteau baritone guitar. Relying on only two microphones to capture a magic blend of room ambience and string detail, Ross sounds intimate and natural. The unprocessed *Passion Session* proves that he is among the best acoustic fretmeisters recording these days.

Klimbim

From the Narada release "Passion Sessions"

Don Ross

Tuning: B'-F#'-C#-F#-B-f#

Notational things: All percussive effects are notated hanging off the bottom line with nonstandard noteheads; square notehead indicates a thump on the face of the guitar with the heel of the right hand; an 'x' notehead is a 'snare' effect produced by bringing down the right thumb or heel percussively onto the strings; the rectangular notehead indicates a quick 'frail' with the right hand while muting the strings with the left; 'H' indicates a hammer-on; 'P' indicates a pull-off; 'SL' indicates a slide; a tie coming out of nowhere indicates a dead-string hammer-on (tap) with the indicated finger; diamond noteheads indicate natural harmonics; vertical straight line arrows indicate a 'frail' strum up or down with the ring finger of the right hand ('anular' in classical notation).

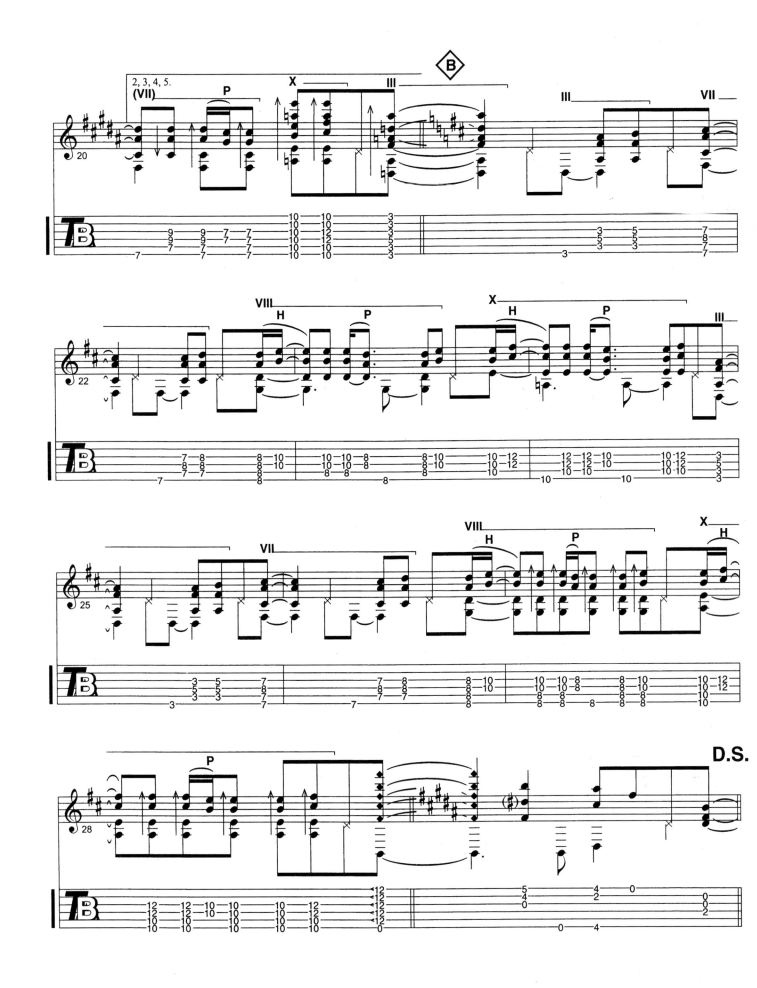

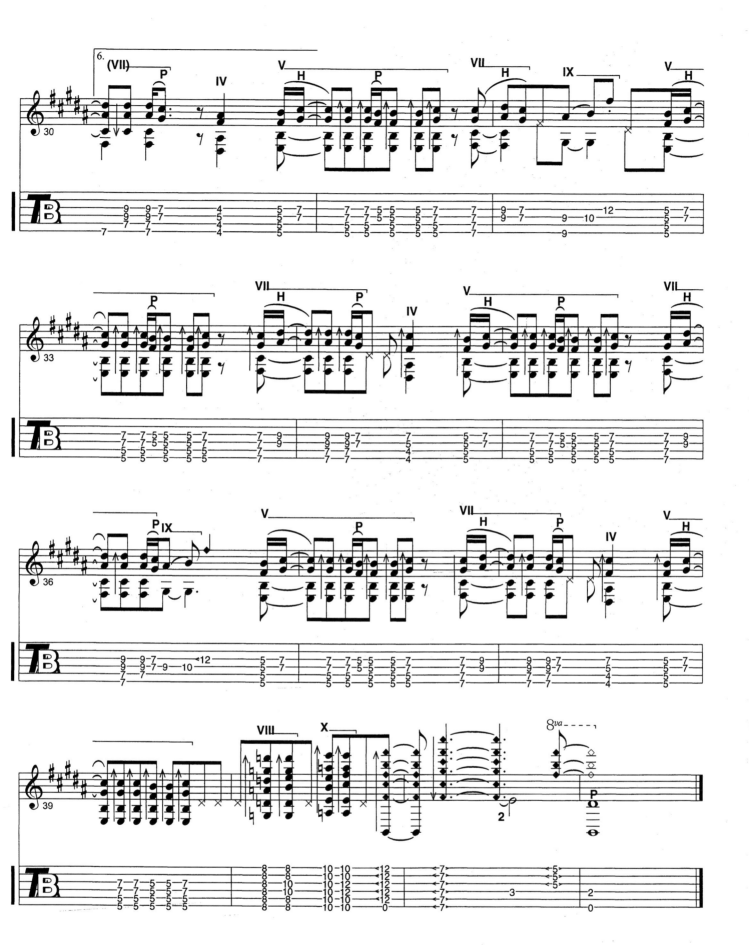

Vincent Sadovsky

Vincent Sadovsky is no stranger to the music industry. In 1973 he opened an acoustic music store in Rochester, Michigan which he and his wife still operate. He has been teaching guitar, banjo, mountain dulcimer and autoharp since 1970, and has become one of the most sought after instructors in Michigan for his composition and technical ability.

Over the years, Vincent has appeared on television and radio broadcasts. His performing has taken him from coffeehouses to festivals, to performing for dignitaries including former president, George Bush. His expertise allowed him to become an "Artist In Residence" for the Michigan Council for the Arts. His passion for acoustic music led him to found and establish the Paint Creek Folklore Society, a nationally known society of acoustic musicians which has been active since 1973. Vincent's playing has enhanced radio and television commercials and documentary films. As a studio musician he has appeared on various recordings.

Since 1976, Vincent has won numerous banjo competitions, and is known for his use of "Keith" tuners. His landmark publication, *New Twists for the Five-String Banjo* sells worldwide.

As a result of Vincent's continued fascination with "Keith" tuners, he has put his banjo aside and developed this technique for the guitar. His use of "Keith" tuners along with his solid finger-style technique adds a new dimension to the art of guitar playing.

Vince's highly acclaimed guitar solo collection, *Guitarscapes* (MB96571BCD) is published by Mel Bay.

Shadow Dancing

Vincent Sadovsky

330

Dylan Schorer

Dylan Schorer lives in the San Francisco Bay area where he formerly worked as the music editor for *Acoustic Guitar* magazine. He records and performs with the Celtic-blues trio Logan's Well along with fellow guitarist Steve Baughman and vocalist Carleen Duncan. He is a respected transcriber of acoustic music and has worked on songbooks for Joni Mitchell, Allison Krauss, Peppino D'Agostino, Neil Young, and Barenberg, Douglas, Meyer.

Glass of Beer

Glass of Beer is a traditional Irish fiddle tune which I've slowed and arranged in the unusual tuning DBDF♯BD. It's essentially open-D tuning (DADF♯AD) with the 5th and 2nd strings tuned up to B, resulting in an open-Bm tuning. On the recording, I'm joined by my good friend Steve Baughman who supplies a rich guitar harmony and counterpoint (not transcribed here).

Glass of Beer

Tuning: DBDF#BD

Traditional Irish, arranged by Dylan Schorer

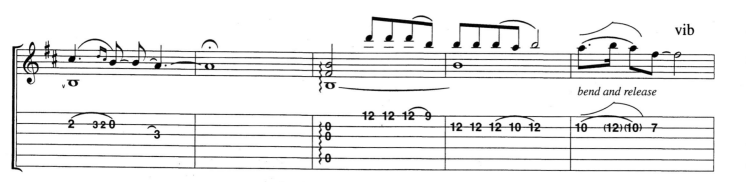

335

A2 *Harmony guitar enters*
(not transcribed here)

337

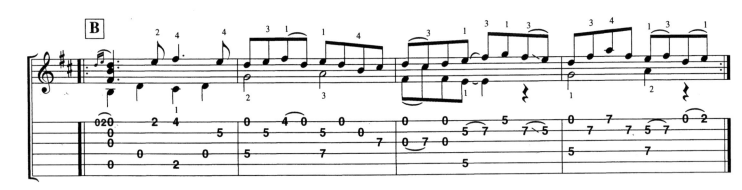

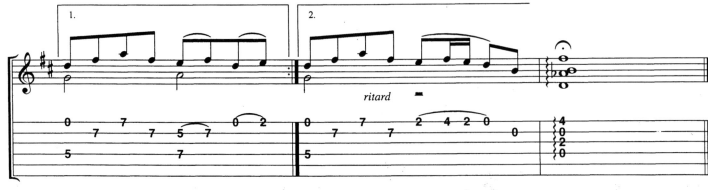

John Sherman

John Sherman has been playing guitar since age ten when, while living in Italy, curiosity led him to pick up a guitar his father had received as a gift. His earliest interest was American folk music, soon followed by classical instruction from Prof. Costas Proakis, a student of Andrés Segovia. Though his exposure to the established and rigorous classical method was all too brief, cut short as it was by his family's return to the U.S., it provided a thorough grounding for the playing style he subsequently developed.

While he has written a few original works, the challenge of arranging existing tunes within the traditional framework continues to engage him: "As long as there are tunes out there to which the guitar can give a unique voice," John says, "I'll be looking for them."

John's solo collection, published by Mel Bay, is titled *So Inclined* (MB96841BCD).

The Rascally Rabbit

Tuning: DADGAD, Capo II
(EBEABE)
E Mixolydian

John Sherman

da Capo

rit (2nd time)

Martin Simpson

English acoustic guitar virtuoso Martin Simpson has come a long way from his roots in Lincolnshire, Northern England. He played his first paid gig at fourteen, became a professional at seventeen, and shortly after found himself in the vanguard on the British folk-rock movement. He has performed with such musical luminaries as Richard Thompson, Steeleye Span and Fairport Convention, as well as working in the Albion Band and for ten years as collaborator and accompanist with June Tabor. More recently he has shared stages with Steve Miller and David Lindley, as well as recording with Ronnie Earl, Bob Brozman, Ed Gerhard and the Chinese pipe player Wu-Man. He continues to record and tour both solo and with his wife Jessica Ruby Simpson.

Martin's dynamic solo guitar performances are legendary, showcasing his mastery of the acoustic guitar as well as his far-ranging repertoire. He possesses a seemingly effortless command of multiple complex styles, including powerful percussive techniques, unique frailing and fingerstyle, and a ground breaking use of open tunings.

Martin's books with Mel Bay include *A Closer Walk with Thee* (MB95285), *Smoke & Mirrors* (MB95717), and his newest, *Cool and Unusual* (MB98383).

Bright Morning Stars

Trad. arr. M. Simpson

Tuning: DADGAD

1st time: guitar
2nd time: guitar
3rd time: violin
4th time: guitar

play 4x

1st time: guitar
2nd time: mandolin
3rd & 4th time: guitar

Watch the Stars

Trad. arr. M. Simpson

Tuning: DADGAD

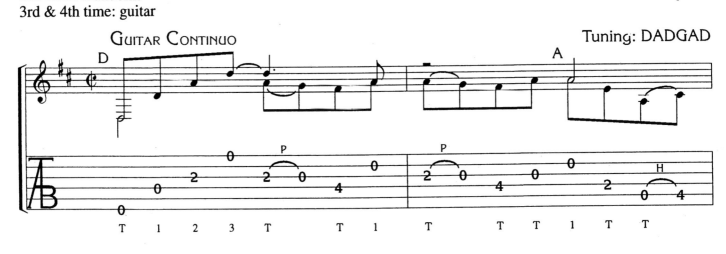

2x (1st time only)

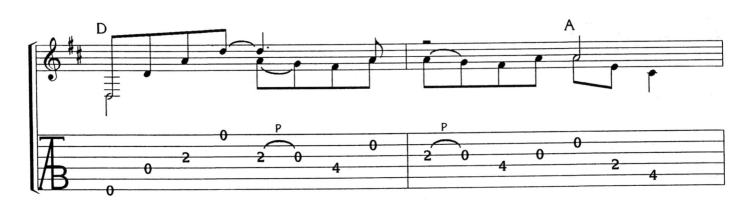

346

Johnny Smith

Johnny Smith, a self-taught guitarist greatly influenced by Andrés Segovia and Django Reinhardt came to prominence in the 1950s with his recording of *Moonlight in Vermont* featuring saxophonist Stan Getz. (*Downbeat* magazine's readers voted the album one of the two best jazz records of 1952). From 1947 to '53, Smith was staff guitarist at NBC Studios, playing guitar and trumpet with both popular and symphonic groups, and writing and performing for many shows, including *Fireside Theater* and *The Dave Garroway Show*.

Aside from the dozen or more of his own recordings for Roost Records, Smith also recorded with Benny Goodman, Hank Jones, and Ray Brown. In the 1960s Smith recorded an original composition *Walk Don't Run*, which the Ventures later transformed into an overnight rock and roll sensation. Striving for a better, unique guitar sound, Smith developed the Johnny Smith Guitar originally manufactured by the Gibson Guitar Company and is now made by Fender/Guild. Since its introduction in 1960, it has been one of the most popular jazz archtop models.

In 1957, at the peak of his influence and popularity as a leader, Smith walked out of the limelight as suddenly as he had entered it, preferring the trout streams of the Colorado mountains to the night-club stage. In fact, Smith says that "the most beautiful sight I ever saw was the New York skyline disappearing in my rearview mirror as I headed West."

The following Johnny Smith guitar solo was transcribed for fingerstyle guitar by classical guitarist, Charles Postlewate.

Waltz

By Johnny Smith
Edited for Classical Guitar
by Charles Postlewate

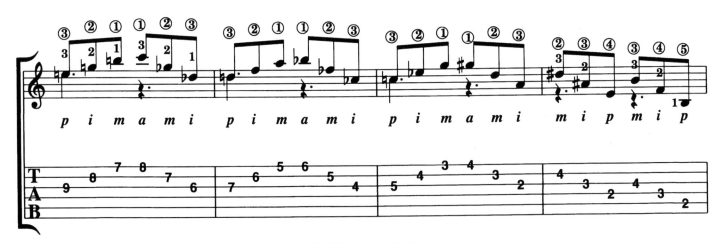

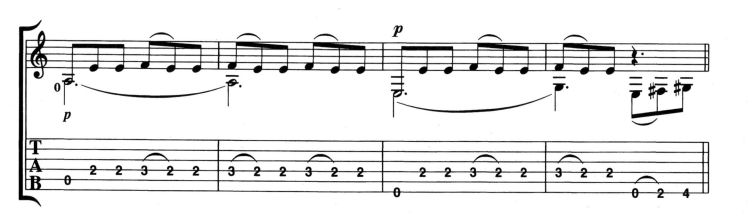

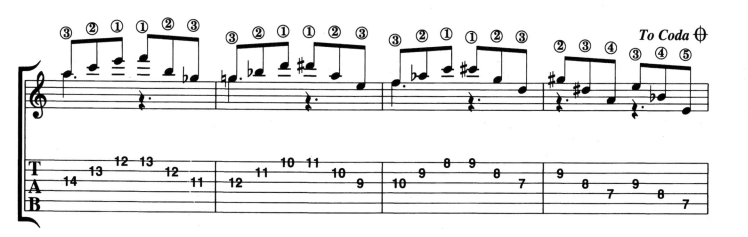

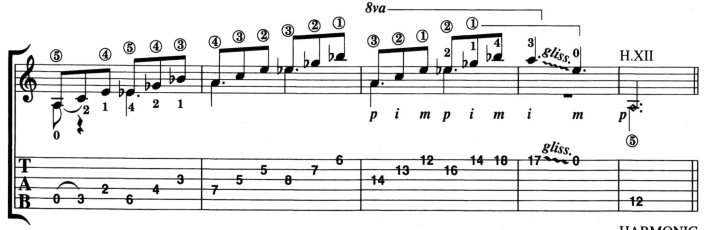

HARMONIC

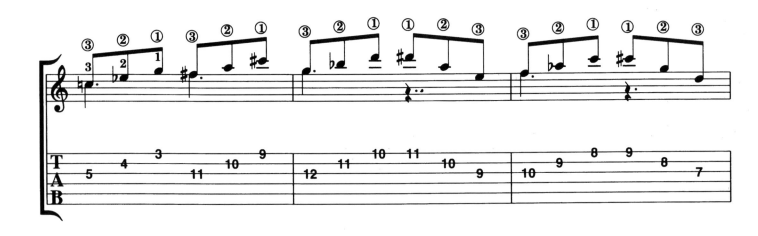

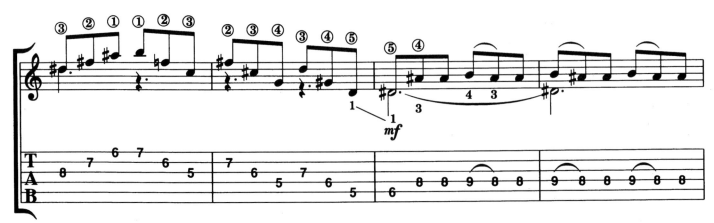

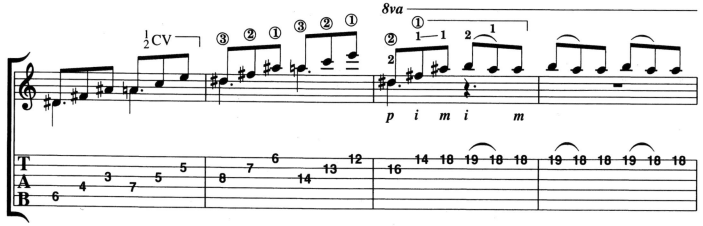

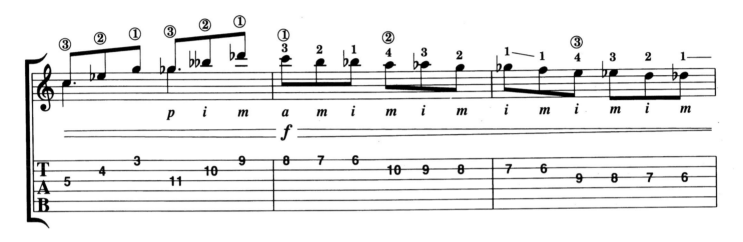

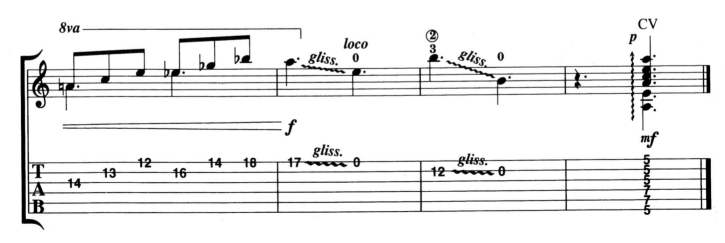

Fred Sokolow

Fred Sokolow is a versatile "musician's musician." A veteran jazz guitarist and singer, he is also an accomplished performer on the 5-string banjo, resonator guitar, and mandolin. Apart from his solo career, Fred has fronted his own jazz, bluegrass, and rock bands, and he has toured with notables such as Bobbie Gentry, Jim Stafford, and the Limeliters. In the recording studio, Sokolow has two recordings that showcases his talents, and he has written more than 50 instructional guitar and banjo books, tapes and videos for seven major publishers. His books, which teach jazz, rock, country and blues, are sold on six continents.

As articulate in person as he is in print, Sokolow presents guitar and banjo seminars across the U.S. You can read reviews of these seminars and of his instructional books and tapes in *Guitar Player* and other music magazines.

Gee

Fred Sokolow

356

Tim Sparks

Tim Sparks' long journey to the 1994 National Fingerstyle Guitar Championship, and beyond, began modestly in Winston Salem, North Carolina, when he started picking out tunes by ear on an old Stella flattop. He was given his first guitar when a bout of encephalitis kept him out of school for a year. The music he heard around him was traditional country blues and the gospel his grandmother played on piano in a small church in the Blue Ridge mountains; that's what he taught himself to play.

A musically astute uncle heard him one day, and amazed that he had come so far on his own, nominated him for a scholarship at the prestigious North Carolina School of the Arts. There he studied the classics with Segovia protegee Jesus Silva while continuing to play all kinds of music, increasingly turning to classic jazz for inspiration. He adapted compositions by Jelly Roll Morton, Scott Joplin, and Fats Waller to the guitar, frequently reducing piano arrangements to their bare essence.

After a stint on the road with a Chicago-based rhythm and blues band, Sparks arrived in Minnesota, where he soon established himself as a journeyman guitarist. While recording three albums with the seminal vocal jazz ensemble Rio Nido, Sparks also became proficient in jazz styles from Brazilian to bebop, earning several regional music awards including Best Acoustic Guitarist, Best Latin Jazz Guitarist, and Best Jazz Guitarist.

He also found the time to revive his interest in the classics, adapting Tchaikovsky's *Nutcracker Suite* to the guitar – a work that has been cited as a significant contribution to solo guitar literature. He also wrote *Balkan Dreams Suite* (MB95449BCD), a remarkable collection of odd-meter guitar arrangements. Many of the Balkan Dreams compositions appeared on Tim's debut solo guitar CD, *The Nutcracker*. The recording was cited by *Guitar Player* magazine as, "An exhilarating, odd-meter minefield inspired by Near Eastern music. An important recording from a gifted composer, arranger and performer."

Fiddle Medley

1/2 CII

John Standefer

John Standefer was born in West Texas in 1950. His childhood interest in music led him to become a professional guitarist and teacher by the age of sixteen. His early influences were Chet Atkins and an eclectic array of folk, jazz, classical and Brazilian players. John's current playing style still reflects this wide variety of interests making his music difficult to categorize to this day. He has a wonderful way of expressing life experiences through his music, however, which is evident in this performance of *Badlands*. When asked about the origins of the piece, John remarked, "This tune paints two distinctly different portraits from the life and times of John Standefer. It is first of all reminiscent of the West Texas of my childhood. I can first picture myself; parched riding a half-dead horse across the hot, endless desert in search of water. Then, as a Christian, *Badlands* figuratively reminds me of my life before finding the Lord. The search was definitely a desert experience in itself, but in the end, led me to the Water of Life."

To learn more about John, his music, Praise Guitar Workshops or his concert schedule, simply check out his website at: www.praiseguitar.com.

Badlands

First of all, tune your guitar to DGDGAD. This Gsus2 tuning provides a modal character to the piece. The effect is augmented by right-hand techniques that add a toughness to the sound. When you see the symbol, < above a set of notes, they are punctuated with a sharp flick of the back of the right hand index fingernail. The arrows indicate strums ↑ = *a downstroke with the back of the nails.* ↓ = *an upstroke (just a brush of the index finger). Note the right-hand technique found at letter A in the intro. This unusual 'grace note' reads 0303 in the tab and is played with a continuous rest stroke across both strings with the index finger, followed by another 'double' rest stroke of the middle finger. I stole this technique from Chet in the '60s and it's still one of my favorite neat little licks – takes a little practice to perfect, but it's worth it.*

–[Badlands] was excerpted from John's CD, [Guitar Stories].

Badlands

John Standefer

369

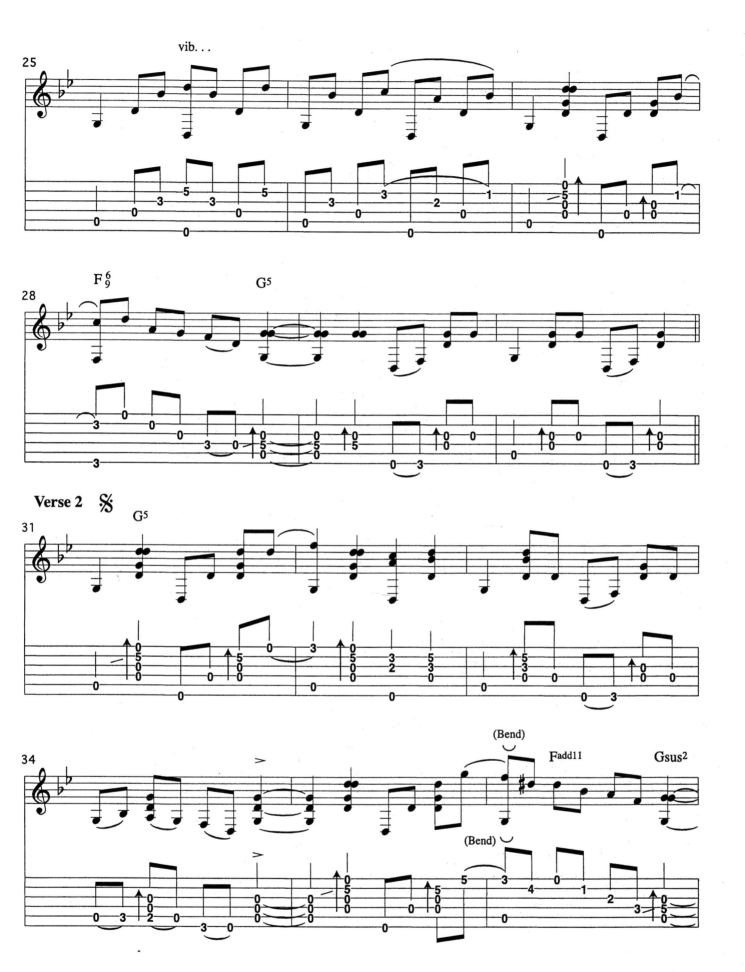

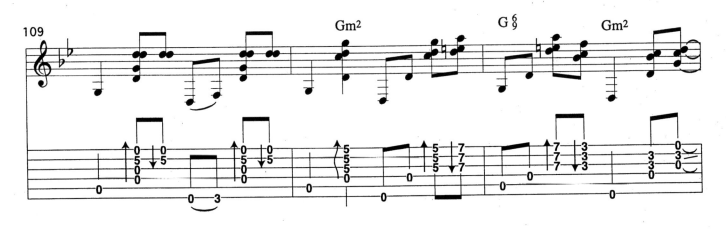

Ending

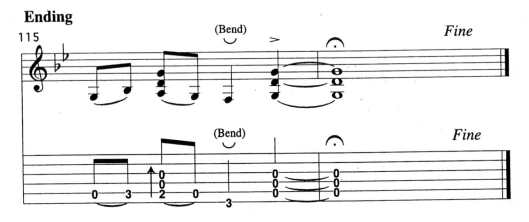

David Surette

Long known as one of a New England's finest acoustic guitarists, David Surette is starting to gain wider recognition for his critically acclaimed solo recordings *Trip to Kemper* and *Black Roads*. "His technique is impeccable" notes *Acoustic Guitar*, "as are his Celtic fingerstyle playing and arranging." Surette is also a top-notch flatpicker on guitar, mandolin, and bouzouki, with a repertoire ranging from Irish and Breton tunes to traditional American roots music and original guitar compositions. In addition to his solo performances, Surette has worked since 1988 with Susie Burke, a wonderful singer of contemporary folk. He's also in demand as a studio musician and free-lance accompanist, working with nationally known acts such as mandolin virtuoso Peter Ostroushko, guitar champ Harvey Reid, and Irish fiddle master Martin Hayes.

In addition to performing and recording, Surette maintains an active teaching schedule, and is head of the folk department at the Concord (NH) Community Music School. He was awarded an NEA travel grant in 1994 to study the traditional music of Brittany, France, and was a 1993 recipient of an Individual Artist Fellowship Award from the NH State Council on the Arts. He has released two albums on the Madrina Music label and has published a book of Celtic guitar arrangements for John August/Mel Bay publications.

Bourrée

Traditional French

Tuning: D A G D A D, Capo 2

Please note - structure is: AABBC AABBC AABB

Additional Music: David Surette

Guy Van Duser

Rounder and Daring recording artist Guy Van Duser is internationally known for his unique stride guitar style of playing, as well as his imaginative and sometimes outrageous arrangements for finger-style guitar, including the amazing *Stars and Stripes Forever*. Mr. Van Duser is a graduate of Oberlin College in music, has twelve recordings available on Rounder, Green Linnet, and Daring Records, as well as many more in collaboration with artists such as Bill Staines and Jeanie Stahl, and is the author of *Stride Guitar* (MB93939BCD) from Mel Bay Publications. As a composer, Guy produces soundtracks for films and public television programs such as *Frontline, Nova,* and *The American Experience.* The documentary film, *Hellfire: A Journey From Hiroshima*, for which Guy composed the music, received an Academy Award nomination. Guy is currently working on *Disney's World of English*, an educational video series designed to teach English as a second language to children in Japan and other Asian countries.

Guy is renowned for his innovative accomplishments on acoustic guitar. Of particular note is his development of what he terms his "stride guitar" technique, a fusion of the finger-picking virtuosity of Chet Atkins with the swing and stride piano styles of Fats Waller, Teddy Wilson, and other jazz pianists of the 1930s. Simultaneously playing bass lines, chords, and melody, he has elevated the swing-style guitar from its traditional rhythmic-accompaniment role and has influenced a new generation of guitarists. He also performs as a two-man big band with clarinetist Billy Novick, and the two are well-known for their unique rendition of classic swing jazz. Guy and Billy are frequently heard on public radio and have often been featured guests on Garrison Keeler's *A Prairie Home Companion*, as well as appearing on *All Things Considered* with Linda Wertheimer. The duo is now celebrating their twenty-third year together.

Cindy and Norm

Guy Van Duser

Transcribed by
Bill Piburn

CD #3
Track #21

slide all the notes

Bend and Release

Bend and Release

Bend and Release

let ring together

Al Viola

My Italian parentage provided me with a musical childhood in Brooklyn, New York. I learned to play all stringed instruments, then later concentrated on the guitar. Then came the formal training and later the professional work.

My first job was in 1945 after being released from the Army. It was with the Page Cavanaugh Trio. That very successful group made many tours throughout the United States, Europe and Canada, as well as making recordings and movies. After that, I worked with some of the big bands such as Harry James, Ray Anthony, Les Brown and Nelson Riddle.

During the time that I was working with the big bands, I was continuing to study the classical guitar. My classical training has paid off when I am asked to accompany and record with many artists such as Frank Sinatra, Peggy Lee, June Christie, Julie London, Steve Lawrence, Neil Diamond, David Clayton Thomas and Rod McKuen.

I first worked with Frank Sinatra in 1947 at the Waldorf Astoria Hotel in New York, then Atlantic Steel Pier after that. In 1962, I went on a world tour with him rasing funds for underprivileged children in each country where we performed. In 1973, I accompanied him at the White House when he performed there. Since then, I have traveled with him the world over again. I have done his television specials and most of his albums (the latest is *Trilogy*). My other television credits include the *Hollywood Palace* and specials with Julie Andrews, Jonathon Winters, Don Knots, and Andy Williams.

My movie credits include *West Side Story, Oklahoma, Who's Afraid of Virginia Wolf, The Godfather, Blazing Saddles*, and many more. It was my guitar that was heard on many TV commercials such as those for *Viceroy, Budweiser*, and many airline themes.

Con Spirito

Con spirito: With spirit and life. All the fingers of the right hand go to work here. Play it with a march feeling and have fun with this prelude.

Paul Yandell

Although semi-retired, Paul Yandell recently completed a Bransong video entitled *Paul Yandell, Fingerstyle Legacy*. At one time he was active as a session player, performing and recording with Hank Thompson, Kitty Wells, Perry Como, Roger Whittaker, Dolly Parton, and on movie soundtracks including *Tender Mercies* and *Every Which Way But Loose*. But Yandell tired of the work when the business began to change. Says Yandell, "In country music, they won't play anything recorded before '86 or before Randy Travis. It's like nobody ever lived before then. The program directors don't worry about what the public wants. They're like the government–they know what's best for you. Besides, everybody wants to play like Albert Lee nowadays. I can't play like Albert Lee. As far as the record business is concerned, thumbstyle guitar playing is about as popular as '61 Chevys. You see one now and then, but most of them are rusty."

As for his days on the road, Yandell comments: "People think it's exciting, but everybody just thinks about getting back home. The best time you have is that hour and a half that you spend on stage. That's where all the fun is. It's not the going and a-coming–that's what wears your butt out. It's better, though, than hauling gravel or working in a tobacco patch!"

Yandell's successes can be attributed to the practice of old fashioned adages. "Listen to everybody and try to be different," he says. "If you ever hear any good advice, take it. All I ever wanted to do when I was a kid was to come to Nashville and play at the Grand Ole' Opry. That was my dream night and day. And the dream eventually came true. Over the years, I've had the opportunities to record with Chet, Les Paul, Jerry Reed. I've played with Merle, Lenny Breau–all my heroes. What more could a guy want? I've really been lucky just to be friends with people like that. And if I can make it, just about anybody can, because I'm just an average talent–not bad, not great, just somewhere in between. Just believe in yourself and try hard enough. Who knows? You might be able to get a job with somebody like Chet."

A complete collection of Paul Yandell's solos may be found in the books *Fingerstyle Legacy* (MB95495BCD) and *Going Home* (MB96460BCD), both published and distributed by Mel Bay.

Relaxin'

Paul Yandell

Andrew York

"A truly gifted guitarist who plays with amazing ease and maturity... his playing always impresses... on his original works the real magic is found..." say critics of guitarist and composer Andrew York. Andrew performs his guitar compositions in solo concerts throughout the United States, Europe and Japan. He is also a member of the internationally recognized Los Angeles Guitar Quartet, whose recent tour schedule includes performances in thirteen countries. LAGQ records for Delos Records International.

Andrew's compositions and arrangements for guitar have gained him wide recognition among both musicians and audiences. Besides his own performances of his works, classical guitarist John Williams has made Andrew's compositions a consistent part of his world-wide concert programing, and recorded *Lullaby* and *Sunburst* on his DBS Records release *Spirit of the Guitar, Music of the Americas*. American guitarists Christopher Parkening and David Brandon feature Andrew's *Evening Dance* on their Angel/EMI recording *Virtuoso Duets,* and Scott Tennnant's debut recording on GHA Records includes some of Andrew's compositions.

Andrew's own discography includes his solo albums *Denouement* on GSP Recordings and *Perfect Sky* on Artifex Records, *Ecstasty,* an album of guitar duos on New World Records, and inclusion on the Windham Hill Records' *Guitar Sampler* and Rhino Records' *Legends of the Guitar-Classical*. Andrew's compositions appear in print worldwide from Guitar Solo Publications in San Francisco and Ricordi in London.

Andrew has been featured on the magazine covers of *Gendai Guitar* in Japan and *Classical Guitar* in England, and interviews with him have also appeared in *Acoustic Guitar* and *Guitar Player* in the US.

Andrew's piece, *Marley's Ghost*, has a captivating reggae feeling. Andrew performs *Marley's Ghost* on the Mel Bay Artist Series Video, *Andrew York/Contemporary Classic Guitar* (MB97257VX). His latest composition, *Three Dimensions for Solo Guitar* (MB97046) is also published by Mel Bay.

Marley's Ghost

Andrew York

(= 128)

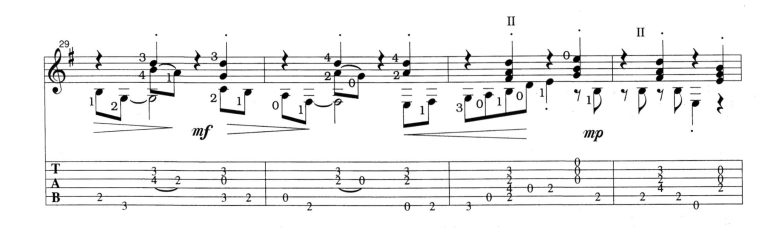

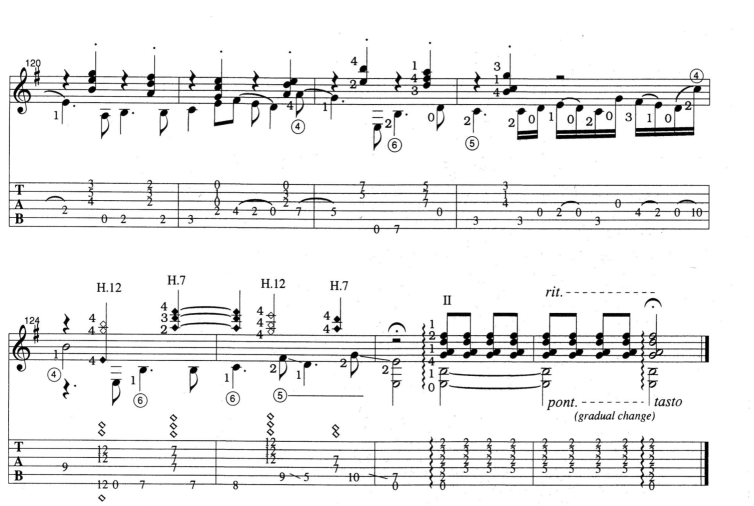

John Zaradin

John Zaradin is Europe's foremost player of classical Brazilian guitar music. His early training at the Royal College of Music and the Paris Conservatoire has combined with his deep involvement and love of the music and people of South America to result in the unique sound he makes today.

John Zaradin holds a Gold Disc for his recording of the *Rodrigo Concerto de Aranjuez* on EMI's Classics for Pleasure series, having sold over a quarter million copies. His other recordings of classical guitar music have included works by Vivaldi, Buxtehude, Cimarosa, Bach and Scarlatti.

After his formal training in London and Paris as a pupil of Alexander Lagoya, John Zaradin began composing and performing his own guitar music in both classical and Brazilian styles. His numerous works are currently published by Belwin-Mills and Hampton guitar Music including the recent index of rhythm patterns—*A Unique Approach to the Study of Rhythm*. John Zaradin has given live television and radio performances in the major musical centers of all five continents.

Over the years, John Zaradin has fused European formality with the spontaneity of Latin America, especially Brazil. His music has been played in concerts with John Dankworth, Paco Pena and other musicians. Brazilian music is now regarded as a valuable source of inspiration to contemporary composers in the same way that European folk music was to such composers as Bartok, Dvorak, and Brahms.

John's Mel Bay books include *Caribbean Fantasy for Acoustic Guitar* (MB96570) and *Latin American Jazz for Fingerstyle Guitar* (MB95556).

Brisas Nordestinas

Brisas starts with a pedal idea over Am7 and moves, at bar 23, onto the second (melodic) section, with chord changes at bar 39. It then uses the pedal as a bridge into the solo section (Am7 D7) at bar 43. Bars 47-54 serve as a scored "ad lib" with some examples of solo ideas. Bar 55 closes the solos and acts as a bridge back into the melody at bar 23 and onto the end at bar 39.

Brisas Nordestinas

John Zaradin

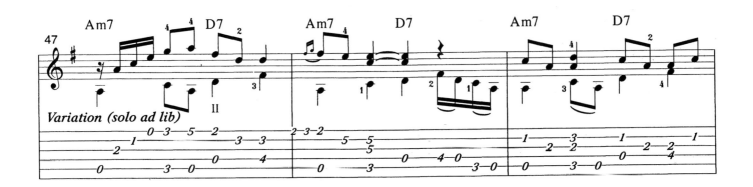

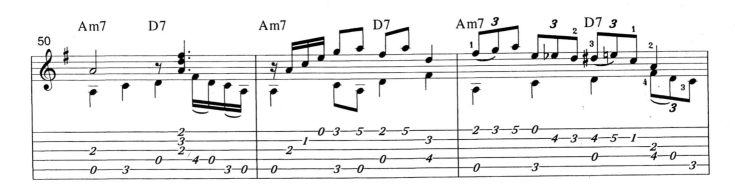

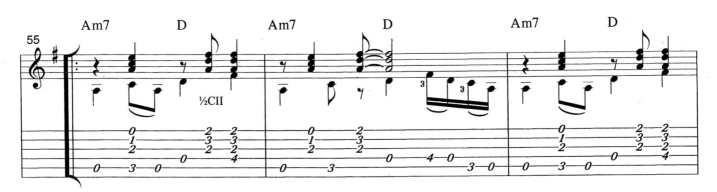

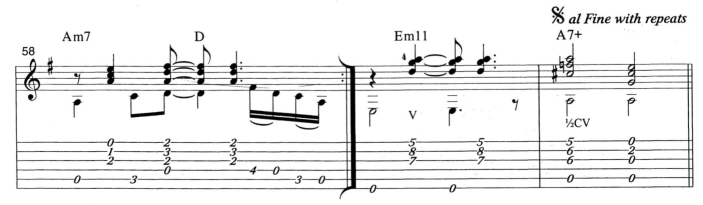